the navajo (diné) native american tribe for kids

Journey into Navajo Culture

sarah michaels

Copyright © 2024 by Sarah Michaels

All rights reserved.

No part of this book may be reproduced in any form or by any electronic or mechanical means, including information storage and retrieval systems, without written permission from the author, except for the use of brief quotations in a book review.

contents

1. WHO ARE THE NAVAJO? 5
   Introduction to the Navajo people 5
   Navajo history and origins 9

2. LIFE IN THE NAVAJO NATION 13
   Navajo Nation today 13
   Traditional and modern Navajo homes (Hogans) 16
   Daily life and family structure 20

3. NAVAJO CULTURE AND TRADITIONS 25
   The Navajo language 25
   Traditional clothing and jewelry 28
   Music and dance 32
   Important ceremonies and rituals 35

4. NAVAJO BELIEFS AND SPIRITUALITY 39
   Navajo spiritual beliefs 39
   The significance of nature in Navajo spirituality 42

5. NAVAJO ART AND CRAFTSMANSHIP 47
   Navajo art forms: weaving, pottery, sand painting 47
   Importance of storytelling and oral traditions 50
   Famous Navajo artists and their contributions 54

6. NAVAJO HEROES AND LEGENDS 59
   Notable Navajo figures 59
   Traditional Navajo legends and folklore 63

7. NAVAJO FOOD AND AGRICULTURE 67
   Traditional Navajo foods and recipes 67
   Farming and livestock practices 71

8. CHALLENGES AND TRIUMPHS 75
　The Long Walk and its impact 75
　Modern-day challenges and achievements 79

9. HOW YOU CAN HELP 83
　Ways to learn more about Navajo culture 83
　How to support the Navajo Nation 87

10. FUN ACTIVITIES AND CRAFTS 91
　Simple Navajo-inspired crafts for kids 91
　Basic Navajo words and phrases to learn 96
　Recipes for traditional Navajo snacks 102

　Glossary 109
　Further Reading and Resources 115

1 /
who are the navajo?

introduction to the navajo people

THE NAVAJO HAVE LIVED in the Southwest for many centuries, but their history stretches back even further. Long ago, the ancestors of the Navajo migrated from what is now Canada to the Southwest. They settled in the region, adapting to its unique landscape and climate. Over time, they developed a rich culture deeply connected to the land and its resources.

Family and community are at the heart of Navajo life. Families often live close to one another in clusters of homes called hogans. A hogan is a traditional Navajo dwelling made from wooden poles, tree bark, and mud. These homes are designed with great care, always facing east to greet the rising sun. This practice is part of the Navajo's spiritual beliefs, emphasizing the importance of harmony with nature and the natural cycles of the earth.

Sarah Michaels

The Navajo people speak Diné Bizaad, a language that is central to their identity. The Navajo language is not only a means of communication but also a way to pass down stories, traditions, and cultural values from one generation to the next. During World War II, the Navajo language played a crucial role when Navajo Code Talkers used it to create an unbreakable code that helped the Allies win the war. Learning about the Navajo language gives us a deeper understanding of their culture and history. For instance, "Yá'át'ééh" means "hello," and "Ahéhee'" means "thank you."

The Navajo have a profound respect for nature, believing that everything in the natural world is interconnected and should be treated with care. This respect is evident in their ceremonies and rituals, which are designed to maintain harmony between humans and nature. One of the most important ceremonies is the Blessingway, which is performed to ensure good fortune and harmony. These ceremonies often include songs, dances, and sand paintings, each with specific meanings and purposes.

Art is an integral part of Navajo culture. Navajo artists are renowned for their beautiful weaving, pottery, and jewelry. Navajo rugs and blankets are famous for their intricate geometric designs and vibrant colors. These items are not just decorative; they tell stories and represent important cultural symbols. Weaving is a skill traditionally passed down from mother to daughter, ensuring that this art form continues through generations. Navajo jewelry, often made with silver and turquoise, is another important cultural expression, showcasing the craftsmanship and creativity of Navajo silversmiths.

Storytelling is a cornerstone of Navajo culture. Through stories, Navajo elders pass down knowledge, values, and history to younger generations. These stories often feature characters like Coyote, a trickster who teaches lessons through his adventures. Listening to these stories, we learn about the Navajo way of life and the values that are important to them, such as respect, community, and living in harmony with nature.

The Navajo have faced many challenges throughout their history. In the 1860s, they were forcibly removed from their homeland and made to walk to a distant area in New Mexico, an event known as the Long Walk. Many Navajo suffered during this journey, but their resilience and strength helped them survive and eventually return to their land. This period of hardship is a testament to the enduring spirit of the Navajo people.

Today, the Navajo Nation is a vibrant community that blends traditional practices with modern life. Many Navajo continue to practice their ceremonies, speak their language, and create beautiful art, while also embracing education, technology, and other aspects of contemporary society. Navajo children go to school, participate in sports, and use the internet, just like kids everywhere else. This blend of tradition and modernity makes the Navajo Nation a unique and dynamic community.

One of the ways the Navajo keep their culture alive is through festivals and fairs. The Navajo Nation Fair, held annually in Window Rock, Arizona, is a celebration of Navajo culture and traditions. The fair features rodeos, parades, traditional dances, and the Miss Navajo Nation pageant. It's an excellent opportunity for Navajo people to come together, share their heritage, and educate others about their way of life.

Food is another important part of Navajo culture. Traditional Navajo foods include fry bread, mutton stew, and blue corn mush. These dishes are not only delicious but also have cultural significance. For instance, fry bread, which is a deep-fried dough, has a complex history tied to the Long Walk and the rations provided by the U.S. government. Despite its origins, fry bread has become a symbol of resilience and adaptability.

The Navajo people have made significant contributions in various fields, from environmental conservation and agriculture to art, science, and politics. Recognizing these contributions helps us appreciate the diverse talents and achievements of Native American individuals and communities. For example, the agricultural practices of Native American tribes have greatly influenced the foods we eat today. Many of the crops they cultivated, such as corn, beans, and squash, are staples in our diets. By learning about these contributions, we can better understand the rich cultural heritage that has shaped our world.

navajo history and origins

The Navajo people have ancient roots that trace back to the Athabaskan-speaking peoples of Canada. Thousands of years ago, their ancestors began a long migration southward, eventually settling in the Southwest United States. This migration is a significant part of their history, as it shaped their identity and connection to the land. The Navajo believe that they emerged from an underworld through a place called Dinétah, which means "among the people" and is considered their traditional homeland.

Once they settled in the Southwest, the Navajo adapted to their new environment, learning to live in harmony with the arid desert landscape. They developed skills in farming, hunting, and gathering, relying on the resources available to them. Corn, beans, and squash, often referred to as the "Three Sisters," became staple crops. These crops were not only essential for their survival but also played a central role in their cultural and spiritual practices.

The Navajo also became skilled shepherds, raising sheep for their wool and meat. Sheep herding and wool weaving became integral parts of their economy and culture. Navajo women, in particular, were renowned for their weaving skills, creating beautiful and intricate rugs and blankets that are highly valued to this day. Each woven piece tells a story, reflecting the weaver's connection to their heritage and the natural world.

Throughout their history, the Navajo have maintained a strong spiritual connection to the land. They believe that the land is alive and imbued with sacred meaning. This connection is reflected in their ceremonies and rituals, which honor the natural elements and seek to maintain balance and harmony. The Navajo have a deep respect for nature, viewing it as a source of life and sustenance.

As the Navajo settled in the Southwest, they interacted with neighboring tribes, such as the Hopi, Zuni, and Apache. These interactions were sometimes peaceful and cooperative, involving trade and cultural exchange, but could also be marked by conflict. The Navajo learned various skills and techniques from these interactions, further enriching their culture and way of life.

The arrival of Spanish explorers in the 16th century brought significant changes to the Navajo way of life. The Spanish introduced new animals, such as horses and sheep, which the Navajo quickly adopted and incorporated into their daily lives. The horse, in particular, transformed Navajo society, enhancing their mobility and ability to trade and interact with other tribes.

However, the arrival of European settlers also brought challenges. The Navajo faced conflicts with Spanish colonizers and later with Mexican and American settlers. These conflicts often resulted in violence and displacement, as settlers encroached on Navajo land and resources. Despite these challenges, the Navajo demonstrated remarkable resilience and adaptability, finding ways to survive and thrive in the face of adversity.

One of the most tragic events in Navajo history occurred in the 1860s, known as the Long Walk. The U.S. government, seeking to control and relocate Native American tribes, forced the Navajo to leave their homeland and march over 300 miles to a desolate area called Bosque Redondo in New Mexico. This forced relocation caused immense suffering, with many Navajo losing their lives due to harsh conditions, lack of food, and disease.

Despite the hardships of the Long Walk, the Navajo's resilience shone through. After several years of struggle and negotiation, they were allowed to return to their homeland in 1868. The Treaty of Bosque Redondo marked a significant turning point, as it recognized the Navajo's right to their land and laid the foundation for the establishment of the Navajo Nation.

Upon their return, the Navajo people worked tirelessly to rebuild their lives and communities. They resumed their traditional practices of farming, herding, and weaving, while also adapting to new circumstances. The resilience and determination they demonstrated during this period are central to their identity and cultural pride.

The 20th century brought further changes and challenges to the Navajo people. The discovery of oil, gas, and other natural resources on Navajo land led to economic opportunities but also brought new conflicts and environmental issues. The Navajo Nation had to navigate complex negotiations with the U.S. government and private companies to ensure that they benefited from these resources while protecting their land and way of life.

During World War II, the Navajo once again demonstrated their strength and ingenuity through the Navajo

Code Talkers. These brave men used their language to create an unbreakable code that played a crucial role in the Allied victory. The Code Talkers' contributions are a source of immense pride for the Navajo people and a powerful example of how their unique cultural heritage has had a significant impact on the broader world.

Today, the Navajo Nation is a thriving community that blends traditional practices with modern advancements. The Navajo continue to speak their language, practice their ceremonies, and create beautiful art, while also embracing education, technology, and other aspects of contemporary life. They are active in various fields, including politics, education, and the arts, contributing to both their community and the wider society.

2 / life in the navajo nation

navajo nation today

THE NAVAJO NATION is not just a piece of land; it's a sovereign nation with its own government, laws, and institutions. The Navajo people, or Diné, govern themselves through a system that blends traditional practices with modern governance. The Navajo Nation Council is the legislative branch, making laws and policies that affect the community. The executive branch is led by the President and Vice President, while the judicial branch oversees legal matters. This structure allows the Navajo to maintain their cultural traditions while effectively managing their affairs in a contemporary world.

Driving through the Navajo Nation, you'll see a mix of modern buildings and traditional hogans. Hogans are still used today, particularly for ceremonial purposes. These traditional dwellings are round and made of wooden poles, tree bark, and mud. They are designed to face east, welcoming the sunrise and symbolizing new beginnings. In contrast, modern homes and buildings are scattered throughout the region, providing a blend of old and new.

Education is a vital part of life in the Navajo Nation. The Navajo place a high value on learning, and there are many schools, both on and off the reservation, that serve Navajo students. Diné College, located in Tsaile, Arizona, is a tribal college that offers a range of academic programs and emphasizes Navajo language, culture, and history. It was the first tribally controlled college in the United States and continues to play a crucial role in higher education for the Navajo people. Navajo Technical University, another important educational institution, offers advanced degrees and technical training, preparing students for a variety of careers.

Healthcare is another essential aspect of the Navajo Nation. The Navajo Area Indian Health Service provides medical services to the community, operating hospitals, clinics, and health programs. Traditional healing practices are also respected and integrated into healthcare, offering a holistic approach to wellness. Medicine men and women continue to play an important role, providing traditional ceremonies and herbal remedies alongside modern medical treatments.

Economically, the Navajo Nation has a diverse landscape. Traditional activities like sheep herding, farming, and weaving remain important, but the Navajo have also embraced various industries to support their economy.

Tourism is a significant source of income, with visitors coming from all over the world to experience the breathtaking landscapes and learn about Navajo culture. Monument Valley, Canyon de Chelly, and the Four Corners Monument are just a few of the many attractions that draw tourists to the area.

In addition to tourism, the Navajo Nation has developed natural resource industries, including coal mining, oil, and natural gas extraction. These industries provide jobs and revenue but also present challenges related to environmental sustainability and the balance between economic development and preserving natural resources. The Navajo leadership works to navigate these complex issues, aiming to protect their land while ensuring economic opportunities for their people.

The Navajo Nation is also a hub of cultural activity. Traditional arts such as weaving, pottery, and silversmithing are thriving. Navajo artists are renowned for their craftsmanship, creating beautiful rugs, jewelry, and pottery that are highly valued both within and outside the community. These art forms are more than just beautiful objects; they carry cultural significance and tell stories of the Navajo way of life.

Music and dance are integral to Navajo culture. Traditional songs and dances are performed at ceremonies and celebrations, often accompanied by the beat of a drum and the sound of a flute. These performances are not just entertainment; they are expressions of cultural identity and spirituality. Modern Navajo musicians also blend traditional sounds with contemporary styles, creating unique and innovative music that reflects their heritage.

Language is a cornerstone of Navajo culture. Diné Bizaad, the Navajo language, is taught in schools and spoken in homes, ensuring that it remains a living and vibrant part of everyday life. Efforts to revitalize and preserve the language are ongoing, with programs aimed at encouraging young people to learn and use Diné Bizaad. This commitment to their language is a powerful way for the Navajo to maintain their cultural identity in a rapidly changing world.

Community is at the heart of the Navajo Nation. Families often live close to one another, supporting each other and maintaining strong ties. The sense of community extends beyond family to include the broader Navajo Nation, where people come together for ceremonies, festivals, and social gatherings. The Navajo Nation Fair, held annually in Window Rock, Arizona, is a major event that celebrates Navajo culture and heritage. It features rodeos, parades, traditional dances, and the Miss Navajo Nation pageant, showcasing the talents and achievements of Navajo women.

traditional and modern navajo homes (hogans)

The word "hogan" comes from the Navajo word "hooghan," which means "home." There are different types of hogans, each serving a unique purpose. The most common is the "female" hogan, which is typically used as a family home. The "male" hogan is used for ceremonial purposes. Let's explore what makes these traditional homes so special.

A traditional female hogan is usually round and built with a framework of wooden poles, covered with tree bark, and sealed with mud. The construction of a hogan is a communal activity, with family and community members coming together to help build it. The door of the hogan always faces east to greet the rising sun, which symbolizes new beginnings and harmony with nature.

Inside a female hogan, you'll find a single room that serves multiple purposes. The central area often features a fire pit, which is used for cooking and heating. The circular design of the hogan represents the Navajo belief in the cycle of life and the importance of balance and harmony. The interior is simple but functional, with rugs and blankets often used for seating and sleeping.

The male hogan, on the other hand, is usually smaller and has a conical shape. It is used for various ceremonies and rituals, such as healing ceremonies, blessings, and initiations. The construction of a male hogan is similar to that of a female hogan, with an emphasis on natural materials and traditional building methods. These ceremonial hogans are sacred spaces where the Navajo connect with their spiritual beliefs and practices.

Building a hogan is not just about creating a shelter; it's a deeply meaningful process that involves prayer and rituals. The construction begins with a blessing ceremony to ensure that the home is built in harmony with the natural world. Throughout the building process, the Navajo people maintain a strong connection to their ancestors and the land, infusing the hogan with cultural and spiritual significance.

While traditional hogans continue to play an important role in Navajo life, modern homes have also become prevalent. These homes often incorporate elements of contemporary architecture and amenities, providing comfort and convenience. However, many modern Navajo homes still reflect traditional values and aesthetics.

In some cases, modern homes are built adjacent to traditional hogans, allowing families to use both types of dwellings. This arrangement provides a blend of old and new, enabling the Navajo to honor their heritage while embracing modern living. For example, a family might use a modern home for everyday activities and a nearby hogan for ceremonies and gatherings.

The evolution of Navajo homes reflects the adaptability and resilience of the Navajo people. They have managed to preserve their cultural identity while navigating the changes brought by modern life. This balance between tradition and modernity is evident in the way Navajo communities are structured, with both types of homes coexisting harmoniously.

The importance of the hogan extends beyond its physical structure. It is a symbol of Navajo culture and a testament to their connection with the land and their ancestors. The hogan represents a way of life that values community, tradition, and harmony with nature. Even as modern homes become more common, the hogan remains a cherished and respected part of Navajo heritage.

Living in a hogan offers a unique experience that connects the Navajo to their cultural roots. It is a space where stories are told, traditions are passed down, and family bonds are strengthened. The hogan serves as a reminder of the Navajo's rich history and their enduring connection to the land.

For children growing up in the Navajo Nation, the hogan is a place of learning and cultural immersion. It is where they hear stories from their elders, participate in ceremonies, and learn about their heritage. This connection to their culture is vital for their sense of identity and community.

In the broader context of Navajo life, the hogan represents the Navajo philosophy of living in harmony with the natural world. The use of natural materials and the east-facing door are just a few examples of how the Navajo integrate their beliefs into their homes. This approach to living is a powerful reminder of the importance of respecting and preserving the environment.

Today, efforts are being made to preserve and promote the use of traditional hogans. Some organizations and community groups offer workshops and programs to teach young Navajo people how to build hogans, ensuring that this important aspect of their culture continues to thrive. These initiatives help keep the tradition alive and provide opportunities for the younger generation to connect with their heritage.

Sarah Michaels

daily life and family structure

Life in the Navajo Nation revolves around close-knit family structures, where multiple generations often live together or near each other. This extended family setup fosters strong bonds and a deep sense of responsibility toward one another. Grandparents, parents, children, and sometimes even great-grandparents share their lives, passing down traditions, stories, and wisdom.

A typical day for a Navajo family starts early. The morning often begins with a prayer or a song, welcoming the new day and giving thanks for the blessings of life. This practice reflects the Navajo's deep spiritual connection to nature and their belief in living harmoniously with the world around them. The family might gather outside their home, facing east to greet the sunrise, which symbolizes new beginnings and the promise of a new day.

Breakfast is a family affair, with everyone pitching in to prepare the meal. Traditional foods like blue corn mush, fry bread, and mutton stew are common, but many families also enjoy modern breakfast staples. Cooking is an important skill in Navajo culture, often taught by elders to the younger generation. This not only ensures that traditional recipes are preserved but also strengthens family ties through shared activities.

After breakfast, the day's activities begin. For many Navajo families, livestock herding is a significant part of daily life. Sheep, goats, and cattle are herded across the expansive landscape, providing meat, milk, and wool. Children often help with these tasks, learning the skills and responsibilities of caring for animals. This hands-on experience teaches them about the importance of hard work, responsibility, and the connection between humans and animals.

In addition to herding, farming plays a crucial role in Navajo life. Families cultivate crops such as corn, beans, and squash, often referred to as the "Three Sisters." These crops are grown using traditional methods that have been passed down through generations. Farming not only provides food but also reinforces the Navajo's bond with the land and their understanding of sustainable living.

Education is highly valued in the Navajo Nation, and children attend school to learn both academic subjects and Navajo language and culture. Schools in the Navajo Nation often incorporate cultural teachings into their curriculum, helping students stay connected to their heritage while preparing them for the future. After school, children might participate in various activities, such as sports, arts and crafts, or traditional dances, further enriching their education and personal development.

Family life for the Navajo is deeply intertwined with cultural and spiritual practices. Ceremonies and rituals are an integral part of their daily lives, marking important events such as births, marriages, and seasonal changes. These ceremonies often involve the entire community, bringing families together in a spirit of unity and mutual support. The Blessingway ceremony, for example, is performed to promote harmony, balance, and good fortune, reflecting the Navajo's holistic approach to life.

Elders hold a revered position in Navajo society, acting as the keepers of knowledge and tradition. They play a crucial role in educating the younger generation about cultural practices, history, and values. Storytelling is one of the primary ways elders pass on this knowledge. Through stories about mythical figures like Coyote, Spider Woman, and the Hero Twins, children learn about their heritage, moral lessons, and the natural world.

In the evenings, families gather for dinner, sharing a meal and reflecting on the day's events. This time together reinforces family bonds and provides an opportunity to discuss any challenges or successes they experienced. After dinner, it's not uncommon for family members to engage in traditional crafts, such as weaving, beadwork, or pottery. These activities are not only a means of artistic expression but also a way to maintain cultural traditions and pass them on to future generations.

Modern life has brought changes to the Navajo Nation, and many families incorporate contemporary conveniences and technologies into their daily routines. Electricity, running water, and the internet are now common in many homes, allowing families to stay connected to the wider world. However, despite these modern influences, the core values of family, community, and tradition remain strong.

The Navajo's connection to their land is evident in their daily activities. Whether it's herding livestock, tending to crops, or participating in ceremonies, the land plays a central role in their lives. This deep connection to the land fosters a sense of stewardship and respect for the environment, guiding the Navajo in their efforts to preserve their natural resources for future generations.

Community events and gatherings are an essential aspect of daily life in the Navajo Nation. Fairs, rodeos, and cultural festivals provide opportunities for families to come together, celebrate their heritage, and enjoy each other's company. These events often feature traditional music, dance, and crafts, showcasing the richness of Navajo culture and strengthening communal bonds.

3 / navajo culture and traditions

the navajo language

DINÉ BIZAAD IS one of the many Athabaskan languages spoken by Native American tribes in North America. What makes it unique is its intricate structure and melodic sounds. For the Navajo people, language is closely tied to their way of life, their stories, and their connection to the land. Speaking Diné Bizaad is a way of preserving their culture and passing it down to future generations.

Learning any new language can be exciting, and Diné Bizaad is no exception. One of the first words you might learn is "Yá'át'ééh," which means "hello" or "it is good." This greeting is often accompanied by a warm smile and a handshake, reflecting the friendliness and hospitality of the Navajo people. Another essential word is "Ahéhee'," which means "thank you." Expressing gratitude is an important part of Navajo culture, and this word is used frequently in daily interactions.

The Navajo language is known for its complex verb system. Verbs in Diné Bizaad are rich with meaning and can convey detailed information about who is doing an action, how it is being done, and even the time and location of the action. This complexity allows speakers to express themselves with great precision and nuance. For example, the verb "níłjool" means "I am walking" and can change form to indicate different subjects and contexts.

One fascinating aspect of Diné Bizaad is its use of tone. Unlike English, where tone mainly conveys emotion or emphasis, Navajo uses tone to change the meaning of words. There are high, low, rising, and falling tones, and getting these right is crucial for clear communication. For instance, the word "bił" with a high tone means "with him/her," while "bìł" with a low tone means "his/her horse." Practicing these tones can be challenging but also a fun way to understand how Navajo speakers hear and produce sounds.

Stories and songs play a vital role in preserving the Navajo language. Elders share traditional tales that teach lessons about life, nature, and the universe. These stories are often told in Diné Bizaad, helping to keep the language alive and vibrant. Children learn these stories from a young age, absorbing not only the language but also the values and wisdom embedded in them. One popular story is about Coyote, a trickster figure who often finds himself in amusing and educational predicaments.

Songs, too, are a powerful way to learn and enjoy Diné Bizaad. Traditional Navajo songs are performed during ceremonies and celebrations, using poetic language and rhythmic patterns. These songs are more than just music; they are expressions of cultural identity and spiritual beliefs. By singing along, children and adults alike connect with their heritage and keep the language vibrant.

During World War II, Diné Bizaad gained international recognition through the heroic efforts of the Navajo Code Talkers. These brave men used their language to create an unbreakable code that played a crucial role in the Allied victory. The code was so effective because Diné Bizaad's complex structure made it impossible for enemy forces to decipher. This remarkable chapter in history highlights the significance and strength of the Navajo language.

Today, efforts to revitalize and preserve Diné Bizaad are ongoing. Many schools in the Navajo Nation incorporate language classes into their curriculum, ensuring that young Navajo people learn to speak and understand their ancestral tongue. There are also immersion programs and online resources available for those who wish to study the language. These initiatives are vital for keeping Diné Bizaad alive and ensuring that it continues to be a cornerstone of Navajo culture.

You might be wondering how you can start learning Diné Bizaad. One way is to begin with simple phrases and greetings, practicing them with friends or family members. You can also listen to Navajo songs and stories, paying attention to the sounds and rhythms of the language. There are online courses and apps designed to teach Diné Bizaad, offering interactive lessons that make learning fun and engaging.

Another great way to learn is by spending time with Navajo speakers. If you have the opportunity to visit the Navajo Nation, try to engage with the local community and practice speaking the language. Navajo people are often happy to share their language and culture with others, and you'll find that even a few words can open up meaningful connections and conversations.

Understanding and speaking Diné Bizaad is a way to show respect for Navajo culture and history. It helps us appreciate the rich tapestry of human languages and the unique perspectives they offer. By learning Navajo, we can also gain insights into the Navajo worldview, their relationship with nature, and their spiritual beliefs.

traditional clothing and jewelry

Traditional Navajo clothing is a beautiful blend of practicality and artistry. It reflects the environment in which the Navajo people live, as well as their cultural values and identity. One of the most iconic items of Navajo clothing is the traditional dress, often made from wool and adorned with intricate patterns. These dresses are typically long, with flowing skirts and a fitted bodice, and are designed to be both comfortable and elegant.

Men traditionally wear a type of woven shirt called a "biil," which is usually made from cotton or wool. These shirts often feature bold stripes or geometric designs, reflecting the natural landscape and cultural symbols of the Navajo Nation. Paired with the shirt, men wear trousers or leggings, completing the traditional look with moccasins made from soft leather.

Women's traditional clothing includes beautiful shawls and skirts, often decorated with vibrant colors and patterns. The designs on these garments are not just for decoration; they hold meanings and tell stories. For example, certain patterns might represent the mountains, rivers, or other natural elements that are important to the Navajo people. These clothes are often worn during ceremonies and special occasions, showcasing the artistry and heritage of the Navajo culture.

The creation of traditional clothing is a communal activity that involves the skills of many people. Wool is often spun and dyed by hand, using natural dyes made from plants and minerals found in the surrounding environment. This process ensures that each piece of clothing is unique and carries the touch of the person who made it. The knowledge of weaving and dyeing techniques is passed down through generations, preserving these traditional crafts.

Jewelry is another essential aspect of Navajo culture, renowned for its beauty and craftsmanship. Navajo jewelry often features silver and turquoise, materials that hold great significance in their culture. Turquoise, in particular, is considered a sacred stone that symbolizes health, protection, and abundance. It is often set in intricate silver designs, creating pieces that are both stunning and meaningful.

The art of silversmithing was introduced to the Navajo in the 19th century, and they quickly mastered and adapted the craft. Today, Navajo silversmiths are highly respected for their skill and creativity. They create a wide range of jewelry, including necklaces, bracelets, rings, and belt buckles, each piece telling a story and reflecting the wearer's identity and heritage.

One of the most recognizable styles of Navajo jewelry is the squash blossom necklace. This necklace features a series of beads and pendants, often with turquoise stones, and ends with a large crescent-shaped pendant called a "naja." The squash blossom design is believed to have originated from Spanish influences, but the Navajo have made it uniquely their own, incorporating traditional symbols and materials.

Another popular item is the concho belt, which consists of large, decorative silver disks (conchos) strung together on a leather belt. These belts are often adorned with turquoise and other gemstones, creating a striking and elegant accessory. Concho belts are worn during ceremonies and special events, showcasing the wearer's status and heritage.

Earrings, too, are an important part of Navajo jewelry. They are often made from silver and turquoise, featuring designs that range from simple studs to elaborate dangly pieces. These earrings are not just for adornment; they also serve as a connection to Navajo culture and traditions.

Wearing such jewelry is a way for Navajo people to express their identity and keep their heritage alive.

Creating Navajo jewelry is a meticulous process that requires great skill and patience. Silversmiths start by melting silver and shaping it into the desired forms. They then set the turquoise or other gemstones, carefully polishing and finishing each piece to perfection. The designs often incorporate traditional symbols, such as animals, plants, and celestial elements, each carrying specific meanings and stories.

The importance of traditional clothing and jewelry goes beyond their physical beauty. These items are integral to Navajo ceremonies and rituals. For instance, during the Blessingway ceremony, participants wear their finest traditional clothing and jewelry to honor the occasion and show respect for the sacred rituals being performed. The clothing and jewelry worn during these ceremonies are often passed down through generations, carrying the stories and spirits of ancestors.

Children in the Navajo Nation also learn about the significance of traditional clothing and jewelry from a young age. They are taught how to weave, sew, and create jewelry, learning the skills that have been passed down through generations. This education is not just about making beautiful items; it's about understanding and preserving their culture and heritage.

Today, while many Navajo people wear modern clothing for everyday activities, traditional clothing and jewelry remain an important part of their cultural identity.

These items are worn with pride during special occasions, ceremonies, and cultural events, serving as a powerful reminder of their rich history and traditions.

music and dance

Music and dance are integral to Navajo life, serving as expressions of their history, beliefs, and values. They are not merely forms of entertainment but are woven into the fabric of ceremonies, storytelling, and everyday activities. Each song and dance has a purpose, whether it's to celebrate, heal, or connect with the spiritual world.

At the heart of Navajo music is the drum. The drumbeat is often referred to as the heartbeat of Mother Earth, symbolizing life and the universe's natural rhythm. Drums come in various sizes, each producing different tones. During ceremonies, the steady beat of the drum provides a foundation for the songs, guiding the dancers and creating a powerful, communal experience.

The Navajo also use a variety of other instruments, each adding unique sounds to their music. The flute, often made from wood, is known for its hauntingly beautiful melodies. Flute music is typically played during more reflective moments and is associated with healing and meditation. Rattles made from gourds, turtle shells, or other natural materials add a rhythmic texture to the music, enhancing the overall experience.

Songs in Navajo culture are more than just musical compositions; they are vessels of history and tradition.

Many songs are passed down orally from one generation to the next, preserving the stories and lessons of the Navajo people. These songs often accompany ceremonies and rituals, such as the Blessingway and the Enemy Way ceremonies, each with its own specific purpose and set of songs.

The Blessingway ceremony, for instance, focuses on bringing harmony and balance to individuals and the community. The songs sung during this ceremony are intended to promote healing and well-being. The Enemy Way ceremony, on the other hand, is performed to cleanse and protect individuals who have encountered negative influences. The songs used in this ceremony are powerful and protective, reflecting the ceremony's purpose.

Dance is equally important in Navajo culture, often performed alongside music to create a complete sensory experience. Traditional dances are rich with symbolism and are performed with precision and grace. One well-known dance is the Yeibichei, or Night Chant, which is part of a nine-night ceremony. Dancers wear elaborate masks and costumes, representing deities and spirits, and their movements are meant to invoke healing and blessings.

Another popular dance is the Ribbon Dance, characterized by its colorful ribbons and joyful movements. This dance is usually performed during celebrations and social gatherings, bringing people together in a spirit of unity and happiness. The dancers move in a circular pattern, symbolizing the cycle of life and the interconnectedness of all things.

The significance of music and dance extends beyond the

ceremonial and social aspects. They are essential tools for teaching and learning. Through music and dance, children learn about their culture, history, and values. They participate in these traditions from a young age, gaining a sense of identity and belonging. Elders play a crucial role in this process, sharing their knowledge and guiding the younger generation.

In addition to traditional forms, contemporary Navajo musicians and dancers are also making their mark. They blend traditional sounds with modern genres, creating unique and innovative music that resonates with both Navajo and broader audiences. Artists like R. Carlos Nakai, a renowned Native American flutist, have brought Navajo music to the global stage, showcasing its beauty and depth.

Modern Navajo bands and musicians often incorporate rock, hip-hop, and other contemporary styles into their music, while still honoring their cultural roots. This fusion not only preserves traditional music but also makes it relevant to younger generations, ensuring that the spirit of Navajo music continues to thrive in new and exciting ways.

Community events and festivals are great opportunities to experience Navajo music and dance firsthand. The Navajo Nation Fair, held annually in Window Rock, Arizona, features performances by traditional and contemporary artists, showcasing the diversity of Navajo music and dance. These events are not only entertaining but also educational, offering insights into the rich cultural heritage of the Navajo people.

For those interested in learning Navajo music and

dance, there are various resources available. Many schools in the Navajo Nation offer classes in traditional music and dance, taught by experienced instructors. Workshops and community programs also provide opportunities to learn and practice these arts. Engaging in music and dance is a wonderful way to connect with Navajo culture and appreciate its depth and beauty.

important ceremonies and rituals

Ceremonies and rituals hold a central place in Navajo culture. They are moments when the community comes together to honor their beliefs, seek healing, and maintain balance and harmony. One of the most significant ceremonies is the Blessingway, known in Navajo as Hózhóójí. This ceremony is designed to promote harmony, balance, and good fortune, essential principles in Navajo life.

The Blessingway is often performed for individuals embarking on a new journey, such as a marriage, birth, or even a new job. It involves songs, prayers, and rituals that aim to ensure the individual's path is smooth and filled with positive energy. A medicine man, or Hataałii, typically leads the ceremony, using sacred herbs, such as corn pollen, to bless the participants and the space. The songs sung during the Blessingway are ancient and powerful, each one carrying the weight of generations of tradition and belief.

Another important ceremony is the Enemy Way, or Nidaa'. This ceremony is performed to cleanse individuals who have encountered negative influences, such as those returning from war or who have experienced trauma. The Enemy Way involves a series of elaborate rituals, including dances, songs, and the creation of intricate sand paintings. These sand paintings are not merely artistic expressions but are believed to be living representations of the spiritual world, created to summon and direct healing energies.

During the Enemy Way, participants engage in a mock battle, symbolizing the fight against negative forces. This ritualistic battle is followed by healing ceremonies that restore balance and peace to the individuals and the community. The ceremony emphasizes the importance of overcoming adversity and emerging stronger and purified.

The Night Chant, or Yeibichei, is another profound Navajo ceremony. This nine-night ritual is one of the most complex and significant healing ceremonies in Navajo culture. It involves elaborate preparations, including the construction of a ceremonial hogan and the creation of sand paintings that depict sacred symbols and deities. The dancers, dressed in masks and costumes representing the Holy People, perform intricate dances that are believed to invoke healing and protection.

The Night Chant is particularly notable for its detailed choreography and the precise execution required of the dancers. Each movement, each step is performed with the intention of aligning the physical and spiritual realms. The ceremony culminates in a night-long chant, where participants sing and pray for healing, balance, and harmony.

The Kinaaldá is a ceremony that celebrates a young Navajo girl's transition into womanhood. This important rite of passage is marked by a series of rituals that honor the girl's growth and potential. During the Kinaaldá, the girl is guided by female relatives and elders, who teach her the values and responsibilities of womanhood. She grinds corn, participates in traditional dances, and receives blessings that are believed to impart strength and wisdom.

The Kinaaldá also includes the baking of a special cake called alkaan. Made from ground corn, the cake is baked in a circular pit and symbolizes the girl's connection to the earth and her community. The ceremony culminates in a race at dawn, where the girl runs towards the east, symbolizing her journey towards a bright and prosperous future.

The Navajo also have ceremonies for agricultural practices, such as the planting and harvesting seasons. These rituals ensure that the crops grow abundantly and that the land remains fertile. The planting ceremony involves prayers and offerings to the Holy People, seeking their blessings for a bountiful harvest. The harvesting ceremony, on the other hand, is a time of gratitude, where the community gives thanks for the gifts of the earth and prepares for the upcoming winter months.

Each of these ceremonies and rituals serves to strengthen the bonds within the Navajo community, connecting individuals to their ancestors, the land, and the spiritual world. They are expressions of a deeply rooted belief in the interconnectedness of all things and the importance of living in harmony with nature and each other.

Participating in these ceremonies requires a deep understanding of Navajo traditions and beliefs. Medicine men

Sarah Michaels

and women, who have spent years learning and practicing their craft, play a crucial role in conducting these rituals. Their knowledge and guidance ensure that the ceremonies are performed correctly and that their intended purposes are fulfilled.

4 /
navajo beliefs and spirituality

navajo spiritual beliefs

CENTRAL TO NAVAJO spirituality is the concept of Hózhǫ́. Hózhǫ́ can be loosely translated as "beauty," but it encompasses much more than that. It represents harmony, balance, and the ideal state of being. Living in Hózhǫ́ means maintaining a balance between the physical, spiritual, and emotional aspects of life. It's about creating and appreciating beauty in the world and ensuring that one's actions contribute to the well-being of the community and the environment.

The Navajo believe that the world was created by the Holy People, who are supernatural beings with great power. These beings include Changing Woman, the Sun God, and the Hero Twins, among others. Each Holy Person has specific roles and responsibilities in the creation and maintenance of the world. Stories about the Holy People are passed down through generations, teaching important lessons and guiding the Navajo in their daily lives.

One of the most important figures in Navajo mythology is Changing Woman. She is a symbol of life and renewal, embodying the natural cycles of birth, growth, and death. Changing Woman is said to have created the Navajo people from the skin on her chest, giving them life and teaching them how to live in harmony with nature. She represents the nurturing aspect of the earth and is honored in many ceremonies and rituals.

The Sun God, or Jóhonaa'éí, is another central figure. He travels across the sky each day, bringing light and warmth to the world. The Sun God is seen as a powerful protector, and his journey across the sky is a reminder of the passage of time and the cycles of nature. Navajo prayers and songs often invoke the Sun God, seeking his blessings and guidance.

The Hero Twins, Monster Slayer and Born-for-Water, are celebrated for their bravery and strength. According to Navajo stories, they were born to Changing Woman and set out on a quest to rid the world of monsters that threatened the Navajo people. Their adventures teach lessons about courage, perseverance, and the importance of protecting the community. The Hero Twins are honored in various ceremonies, and their stories are told to inspire and educate young Navajo.

The Navajo also have a deep respect for the natural world, believing that everything in nature has a spirit. This includes the earth, water, mountains, and animals. The

Navajo view the land as sacred and see themselves as its caretakers. This spiritual connection to the land is evident in their agricultural practices, where they use traditional methods that honor and preserve the environment.

Water is considered especially sacred, and its presence is vital in many Navajo ceremonies. Water represents life and is used in purification rituals to cleanse the body and spirit. Springs, rivers, and lakes are treated with great reverence, and prayers are often offered to ensure the continued flow and purity of water sources.

The Navajo also believe in the existence of malevolent spirits or "skinwalkers." These are witches who can transform into animals and cause harm to others. The fear of skinwalkers is deeply ingrained in Navajo culture, and stories about them are often told to caution against negative behaviors and to reinforce the importance of living in harmony and balance.

Ceremonies and rituals play a crucial role in Navajo spiritual life, serving as a way to connect with the Holy People and the natural world. These ceremonies often involve chants, prayers, and the use of sacred objects like corn pollen and herbs. Medicine men and women, who are highly respected in Navajo society, lead these ceremonies and use their knowledge of herbs, chants, and rituals to heal and guide the community.

One such ceremony is the Mountain Chant, a nine-day ritual performed to restore balance and harmony. It involves complex chants, dances, and sand paintings, which are believed to invoke the Holy People and bring healing to the participants. The sand paintings, created from colored sands, depict sacred symbols and serve as portals to the spiritual world. After the ceremony, the sand paintings are destroyed, symbolizing the release of the healing powers into the world.

Another important ceremony is the Wind Chant, which is performed to bring rain and ensure a good harvest. The Navajo believe that the wind is a powerful force that can bring both blessings and challenges. The Wind Chant involves songs and prayers that call upon the wind to bring rain and prosperity. This ceremony highlights the Navajo's deep connection to the elements and their reliance on nature for survival.

Navajo spirituality also emphasizes the importance of personal responsibility and ethical behavior. The concept of K'é, or kinship, teaches that everyone is connected and that individuals have a duty to care for their family, community, and the environment. This sense of interconnectedness fosters a strong sense of community and encourages actions that promote harmony and balance.

the significance of nature in navajo spirituality

The Navajo people believe that everything in nature has a spirit, known as a Diyin Diné'é. This belief in the spiritual essence of nature fosters a deep respect and reverence for the environment. The earth, mountains, rivers, plants, and animals are all seen as interconnected and essential to the balance and harmony of the world. This interconnectedness is a fundamental principle of Navajo spirituality, guiding their actions and interactions with the natural world.

The four sacred mountains are particularly significant in Navajo spirituality. These mountains—Mount Blanca in Colorado, Mount Taylor in New Mexico, the San Francisco Peaks in Arizona, and Mount Hesperus in Colorado—mark the traditional boundaries of the Navajo homeland, known as Dinétah. Each mountain is associated with a cardinal direction, a color, and specific spiritual attributes. For instance, Mount Blanca, located to the east, is associated with the color white and represents the dawn, new beginnings, and the element of air.

These sacred mountains are not only geographical landmarks but also spiritual anchors that provide a sense of place and identity for the Navajo people. They are often invoked in prayers, songs, and ceremonies, emphasizing their importance in maintaining balance and harmony. Climbing or visiting these mountains is considered a pilgrimage, an act of connecting with the sacred and seeking blessings and guidance from the Holy People.

Water is another essential element in Navajo spirituality. Springs, rivers, and lakes are considered sacred and are treated with great reverence. Water is seen as a source of life and purification, used in various ceremonies to cleanse and bless individuals and spaces. The Navajo have specific rituals for collecting and using water, ensuring that it is respected and honored as a precious resource. Prayers and offerings are often made to water sources to express gratitude and seek continued blessings.

Plants and animals also hold significant spiritual meaning. Each plant and animal is believed to have its own spirit and role in the ecosystem. Medicinal plants, for example, are used in healing ceremonies, with each plant chosen for its specific properties and spiritual significance. The gathering of these plants is done with great care and respect, often accompanied by prayers and offerings to thank the spirits of the plants for their healing gifts.

Animals are also revered in Navajo culture, with certain animals being considered sacred or symbolic. The eagle, for example, is seen as a messenger between the earthly and spiritual realms, and its feathers are used in many ceremonies to bring blessings and protection. The coyote, despite its trickster reputation, is respected for its intelligence and adaptability. The stories and teachings about these animals often carry important moral lessons and cultural values.

The natural cycles of the seasons are closely observed and celebrated in Navajo spirituality. Each season brings its own set of rituals and ceremonies that align with the changes in the environment. Spring, for example, is a time of renewal and planting, marked by ceremonies that celebrate new life and growth. Summer brings the harvest, with rituals to give thanks for the abundance of the earth. Fall is a time of preparation and reflection, while winter is a period of rest and storytelling, when the Navajo gather to share their oral traditions and strengthen their community bonds.

The significance of nature in Navajo spirituality is also reflected in their architectural practices. Traditional hogans, the primary dwellings of the Navajo, are built in harmony with the natural world. The door of the hogan always faces east, greeting the rising sun and welcoming new beginnings. The circular shape of the hogan represents the cyclical nature of life and the importance of balance and unity. The construction of a hogan is a communal effort, often accompanied by rituals and prayers to ensure harmony and protection for its inhabitants.

Nature is not only a source of spiritual guidance but also a teacher for the Navajo people. The natural world is seen as a source of wisdom, offering lessons on how to live in harmony and balance. Observing the behavior of animals, the growth patterns of plants, and the changes in the weather all provide insights into the rhythms of life and the interconnectedness of all things. This deep relationship with nature fosters a sense of humility and respect, encouraging the Navajo to live in a way that honors and sustains the environment.

The Navajo also have specific ceremonies to honor and connect with nature. The Blessingway ceremony, for example, seeks to harmonize and balance the individual with the natural world, ensuring that they live in Hózhǫ́, or beauty and harmony. This ceremony involves prayers, songs, and rituals that invoke the spirits of nature and the Holy People, seeking their blessings and guidance.

5 /
navajo art and craftsmanship

navajo art forms: weaving, pottery, sand painting

WEAVING IS PERHAPS one of the most well-known and cherished Navajo art forms. Navajo weavers are renowned for their skill and creativity, producing rugs and blankets that are admired worldwide. The art of weaving has been passed down through generations, with techniques and designs evolving over time while maintaining their traditional roots.

The process of weaving begins with the preparation of the wool. Sheep are sheared, and the wool is cleaned, carded, and spun into yarn. This yarn is then dyed using natural dyes made from plants, minerals, and other natural materials. Each color carries its own significance, with earthy tones reflecting the natural landscape of the Navajo Nation.

Sarah Michaels

The actual weaving is done on a vertical loom, a technique that requires patience and precision. Navajo weavers often create intricate geometric patterns and symbols that tell stories or represent elements of their culture. For example, the diamond shape might represent the sacred mountains, while zigzag lines could symbolize lightning. Each rug or blanket is a unique creation, a blend of artistry and cultural expression.

Weaving is not just a craft; it's a way of life that connects the weaver to their ancestors and their heritage. The act of weaving is often accompanied by songs and prayers, infusing the process with spiritual significance. The final product is more than just a textile; it is a piece of art that embodies the weaver's skill, creativity, and cultural identity.

Pottery is another essential Navajo art form, though it is less well-known than weaving. Navajo pottery is distinct for its simplicity and functionality, often featuring beautiful yet understated designs. Traditional Navajo pottery is made using hand-coiled techniques, where clay is shaped into pots without the use of a potter's wheel.

The clay is gathered from specific locations that are considered sacred, and the process of making pottery is filled with rituals and prayers. Once the clay is shaped into the desired form, it is left to dry and then fired in an outdoor kiln. The firing process can be quite challenging, as it requires precise control of temperature and timing to achieve the right finish.

Navajo pottery often features designs that are inspired by nature and the surrounding environment. Common motifs include rain, clouds, animals, and plants. These designs are not just decorative; they carry meanings and stories that reflect the Navajo way of life. For example, a pot with rain symbols might be used in ceremonies to bring rain and ensure a good harvest.

While traditional Navajo pottery was primarily functional, used for storing food and water, contemporary Navajo potters also create pieces that are intended for artistic expression. These modern pieces often incorporate traditional techniques and designs but are crafted to be appreciated as works of art.

Sand painting is one of the most unique and spiritually significant Navajo art forms. Unlike weaving and pottery, sand paintings are not created to be permanent. Instead, they are intricate designs made from colored sand, used primarily in healing ceremonies. These sand paintings are created by medicine men, who use them to invoke the Holy People and bring healing to individuals and the community.

The process of creating a sand painting is a sacred act. It begins with the preparation of the sand, which is colored using natural pigments. The medicine man then carefully places the sand onto a smooth surface, creating detailed images that represent deities, animals, and other symbols. The designs are often symmetrical and filled with vibrant colors, each chosen for its specific meaning and purpose.

Sand paintings are used in ceremonies such as the Night Chant and the Blessingway, where they serve as portals to the spiritual world. The images are believed to draw in the

Holy People, who bring their healing powers to the participants. Once the ceremony is complete, the sand painting is destroyed, symbolizing the release of the healing energies into the world.

Each of these art forms— weaving, pottery, and sand painting—plays a vital role in Navajo culture. They are more than just artistic expressions; they are ways of preserving and passing down traditions, stories, and values. Through their art, the Navajo people connect with their ancestors, their land, and their spiritual beliefs.

For children and young people, learning these art forms is a way to connect with their heritage and develop a sense of identity and pride. Elders and skilled artists teach the younger generation, ensuring that these traditions continue to thrive. The process of learning and creating art is also a way to build community, as families and communities come together to share knowledge and celebrate their culture.

By exploring Navajo art, we gain insight into the rich and vibrant culture of the Navajo people. We see how their creativity is intertwined with their spirituality, their environment, and their history. Each piece of art, whether a woven rug, a pottery vessel, or a sand painting, tells a story and carries a piece of the Navajo soul.

importance of storytelling and oral traditions

Storytelling is a cornerstone of Navajo culture. It is through stories that the Navajo people pass down their history, beliefs, values, and traditions from one generation to the next. These stories are not just for entertainment; they are educational tools that teach important lessons about life, nature, and the universe. The role of the storyteller is highly respected, and the stories themselves are regarded as living entities that carry the spirit and knowledge of the ancestors.

One of the most well-known figures in Navajo storytelling is Coyote, or Ma'ii. Coyote is a trickster and a shape-shifter, often getting into trouble and causing chaos. However, his stories are filled with valuable lessons about the consequences of reckless behavior, the importance of wisdom, and the complexities of human nature. Through Coyote's adventures and misadventures, listeners learn about the importance of making good choices and the impact of their actions on the world around them.

Another significant character in Navajo stories is Changing Woman, or Asdzáá Nádleehi. She represents life, growth, and renewal. Her stories teach about the cycles of nature, the importance of nurturing life, and the role of women in Navajo society. Changing Woman is a symbol of resilience and the enduring spirit of the Navajo people, showing how they adapt and thrive through changing times.

The Hero Twins, Monster Slayer (Naayéé' Neizghání) and Born-for-Water (Tóbájíshchíní), are also central figures in Navajo mythology. Their tales of bravery and heroism are told to inspire courage and perseverance. The Hero Twins set out to protect their people from monsters and dangers, symbolizing the fight against adversity and the importance of standing up for what is right. These stories highlight the values of bravery, loyalty, and the protection of community.

Navajo stories are often rich with symbolism and layers of meaning. They incorporate elements of the natural world, such as animals, plants, and celestial bodies, each carrying specific messages and teachings. For example, the eagle is seen as a messenger of the Holy People, representing strength and vision. Stories involving eagles often emphasize the importance of clarity, perspective, and spiritual connection.

The act of storytelling itself is a communal experience that brings people together. It creates a shared space where listeners can connect with their cultural heritage and with each other. Elders, who are the primary storytellers, play a crucial role in this process. They are the keepers of knowledge, and their stories are a bridge between the past and the present. Through storytelling, elders pass on their wisdom and ensure that the cultural identity of the Navajo people is preserved.

Oral traditions are not limited to stories; they also include songs, prayers, and chants. These oral practices are integral to Navajo ceremonies and rituals, invoking the presence of the Holy People and the spirits of nature. Songs and chants are performed to bring healing, protection, and blessings, reinforcing the spiritual connections that underpin Navajo life. The words and melodies of these songs carry the power of the ancestors, connecting the Navajo to their history and their land.

In addition to their cultural and spiritual significance, storytelling and oral traditions are educational tools. They teach language, history, geography, and moral values. Through stories, children learn about their ancestors, their community, and the world around them. They develop language skills, listening abilities, and critical thinking. Oral traditions provide a holistic education that encompasses both the mind and the spirit.

The preservation of storytelling and oral traditions is vital in maintaining the Navajo language. Diné Bizaad, the Navajo language, is an integral part of these oral practices. Telling stories in Diné Bizaad helps keep the language alive and ensures that it is passed down to future generations. It also reinforces cultural identity and pride, reminding the Navajo of their rich heritage and the beauty of their language.

Modern technology and media have provided new platforms for preserving and sharing Navajo stories and oral traditions. Recordings of elders telling stories, digital archives of songs and chants, and online educational programs all play a role in keeping these traditions vibrant. These modern tools complement the traditional practices, making it easier for younger generations to access and learn from their cultural heritage.

Despite the challenges of modernization and cultural assimilation, the Navajo people have shown remarkable resilience in preserving their storytelling traditions. Community events, cultural festivals, and educational programs continue to celebrate and promote these practices.

Sarah Michaels

Storytelling remains a living tradition, adapting to contemporary contexts while staying rooted in ancient wisdom.

famous navajo artists and their contributions

One of the most renowned Navajo artists is R.C. Gorman, often referred to as the "Picasso of American Indian artists." Born in 1931 in Chinle, Arizona, Gorman grew up surrounded by the natural beauty of the Navajo Nation, which deeply influenced his artistic style. He is best known for his paintings and sculptures of Native American women, capturing their grace, strength, and beauty. Gorman's use of vibrant colors and flowing lines reflects the landscapes and cultural richness of his homeland. His works have been exhibited in prestigious galleries and museums around the world, bringing Navajo art to a global audience.

Gorman's contributions extend beyond his art; he was also a passionate advocate for Native American rights and education. He established the R.C. Gorman Navajo Gallery in Taos, New Mexico, which showcases not only his work but also that of other Native American artists. Through his art and advocacy, Gorman has played a crucial role in promoting Native American culture and providing a platform for indigenous voices in the art world.

Another influential Navajo artist is Shonto Begay, known for his evocative paintings that depict the everyday life and spiritual essence of the Navajo people. Born in 1954 in a traditional hogan near Shonto, Arizona, Begay grew up immersed in Navajo traditions and storytelling. His art reflects this upbringing, blending realistic and abstract elements to create powerful narratives. Begay's paintings often feature rich textures and earthy tones, capturing the spirit of the Navajo land and people.

Begay's work is deeply personal and often addresses social and environmental issues affecting Native American communities. His painting "Life on the Reservation" is a poignant portrayal of the challenges and resilience of the Navajo people, highlighting themes of identity, survival, and hope. Begay's art has been exhibited in numerous galleries and is included in several prestigious collections. He also works as an educator, sharing his knowledge and inspiring young Navajo artists to explore their creative potential.

The legacy of Navajo art is also carried forward by artists like Elouise Tso, a master weaver who has dedicated her life to preserving and promoting the traditional Navajo art of weaving. Tso's intricate rugs and blankets are renowned for their precision and beauty, each piece telling a story through its patterns and colors. Born in 1934 in Tuba City, Arizona, Tso learned the art of weaving from her mother and grandmother, continuing a tradition that has been passed down through generations.

Tso's contributions to Navajo art go beyond her own creations. She has taught weaving to countless students, ensuring that this important cultural practice remains vibrant and relevant. Her work has been featured in exhibitions and publications, showcasing the skill and artistry of Navajo weavers. Through her dedication to teaching and her exceptional craftsmanship, Tso has played a vital role in preserving Navajo culture and inspiring new generations of artists.

Navajo jewelry-making is another field where talented artists have made significant contributions. Tommy Singer, a celebrated silversmith, was known for his innovative designs and masterful craftsmanship. Born in 1940 in Winslow, Arizona, Singer came from a long line of silversmiths and began learning the craft at a young age. He is credited with pioneering the "chip-inlay" technique, which involves embedding crushed turquoise and coral into silver, creating striking patterns and textures.

Singer's jewelry is highly sought after and is characterized by its bold designs and meticulous attention to detail. His pieces often incorporate traditional Navajo symbols and motifs, blending them with contemporary styles. Singer's work has been exhibited in galleries and museums and is cherished by collectors around the world. His legacy continues through his family, who have carried on the tradition of Navajo silversmithing.

Another notable Navajo jeweler is Ella Mae Begay, whose intricate silver and turquoise jewelry has earned her acclaim and admiration. Born in 1952 in Tohatchi, New Mexico, Begay learned the art of jewelry-making from her mother and has developed her own distinctive style. Her work often features traditional Navajo symbols, such as the bear, eagle, and corn, which hold deep spiritual significance. Begay's jewelry is celebrated for its elegance and craftsmanship, reflecting the beauty and heritage of the Navajo people.

The contributions of Navajo artists extend beyond their individual works; they also play a crucial role in promoting and preserving Navajo culture. Through their art, they tell stories, express their identity, and share their experiences with the world. They inspire young Navajo artists to explore their creative potential and take pride in their cultural heritage.

Organizations and institutions also support the work of Navajo artists, providing platforms for their art and opportunities for collaboration and education. The Navajo Nation Museum, located in Window Rock, Arizona, showcases the work of Navajo artists and provides a space for cultural exchange and learning. The museum hosts exhibitions, workshops, and events that celebrate Navajo art and culture, fostering a deeper understanding and appreciation of this rich artistic tradition.

6 /
navajo heroes and legends

notable navajo figures

ONE OF THE most revered leaders in Navajo history is Manuelito, known for his bravery and dedication to his people. Born in 1818 in the Bear's Ear region of Utah, Manuelito grew up in a time of great turmoil. The Navajo were facing increasing pressure from settlers and the U.S. government, leading to conflicts and the eventual forced relocation known as the Long Walk.

Manuelito emerged as a strong and visionary leader, advocating for his people's rights and fighting to protect their land and way of life. He is best known for his role during the Navajo Wars, where he led resistance efforts against U.S. military forces. His courage and strategic skills were instrumental in many battles, earning him respect and admiration among the Navajo.

One of Manuelito's most significant contributions was

his leadership during the Long Walk of 1864. When the U.S. government forcibly removed the Navajo from their homeland, Manuelito and thousands of Navajo were marched over 300 miles to Bosque Redondo, a desolate reservation in New Mexico. The conditions were harsh, and many Navajo suffered and died during the journey and while living at Bosque Redondo.

Despite these hardships, Manuelito remained steadfast in his resolve to return to their ancestral land. He tirelessly negotiated with the U.S. government, advocating for the rights and well-being of his people. In 1868, his efforts bore fruit when the Treaty of Bosque Redondo was signed, allowing the Navajo to return to a portion of their homeland. This triumph was a testament to Manuelito's unwavering dedication and leadership, and his legacy continues to inspire the Navajo people.

Another group of remarkable Navajo figures are the Navajo Code Talkers, whose contributions during World War II were both innovative and invaluable. The idea to use the Navajo language as a code came from Philip Johnston, the son of a missionary who had grown up on the Navajo reservation. Johnston recognized the potential of the complex and unwritten Navajo language as an unbreakable code.

In 1942, the first group of 29 Navajo men were recruited by the U.S. Marine Corps to develop this code. These men, known as the original Code Talkers, created a system that used Navajo words to represent military terms. For example, the Navajo word for "turtle" was used to signify a tank, and "chicken hawk" represented a dive bomber.

The Navajo Code Talkers were deployed to various battlefields in the Pacific, including Iwo Jima, Okinawa, and Guadalcanal. Their code was used to transmit vital messages that were crucial to the success of military operations. Despite the intense pressure and danger they faced, the Code Talkers carried out their duties with exceptional skill and bravery.

One of the most famous stories involving the Navajo Code Talkers took place during the Battle of Iwo Jima. Major Howard Connor, the 5th Marine Division's signal officer, famously stated, "Were it not for the Navajos, the Marines would never have taken Iwo Jima." The Code Talkers transmitted over 800 messages without error, playing a pivotal role in the success of the operation.

The contributions of the Navajo Code Talkers remained classified for many years, and their heroism went unrecognized until the declassification of their mission in 1968. In 2001, President George W. Bush awarded the original Code Talkers the Congressional Gold Medal, acknowledging their vital role and honoring their service. The legacy of the Navajo Code Talkers is a powerful example of how the unique aspects of Navajo culture and language were used to serve and protect the nation.

Moving from the battlefield to the world of art and culture, another notable figure is R.C. Gorman, a celebrated Navajo artist known for his paintings and sculptures. Born in 1931 in Chinle, Arizona, Gorman was deeply influenced by the natural beauty of the Navajo Nation and the rich cultural traditions of his people. His artwork, which often features Native American women, is renowned for its vibrant colors and fluid lines.

Gorman's contributions to the art world extend beyond his creative works. He played a crucial role in bringing Native American art to a broader audience, helping to break down barriers and promote cultural understanding. Through his art and advocacy, Gorman celebrated the beauty and strength of Navajo culture, inspiring many and leaving a lasting legacy.

Another influential Navajo artist is Shonto Begay, whose paintings vividly depict the daily life and spiritual essence of the Navajo people. Born in 1954 in a traditional hogan near Shonto, Arizona, Begay grew up immersed in Navajo traditions and storytelling. His art blends realistic and abstract elements, capturing the spirit and resilience of his people.

Begay's work often addresses social and environmental issues, reflecting his deep connection to his culture and his commitment to advocacy. His painting "Life on the Reservation" offers a poignant look at the challenges faced by the Navajo people, emphasizing themes of survival, identity, and hope. Through his art, Begay continues to educate and inspire, fostering a greater appreciation for Navajo culture.

In the realm of education and leadership, Annie Wauneka stands out as a trailblazer. Born in 1910, Wauneka was the daughter of the Navajo leader Chee Dodge. She became a prominent health advocate and educator, dedicating her life to improving the health and well-being of the Navajo people. Wauneka served on the Navajo Tribal Council and worked tirelessly to combat diseases such as tuberculosis.

Her efforts in health education and public health initiatives earned her national recognition, including the Presidential Medal of Freedom in 1963. Wauneka's work has had a lasting impact on the Navajo Nation, improving health outcomes and empowering future generations to continue her legacy of service and leadership.

traditional navajo legends and folklore

One of the most well-known figures in Navajo folklore is Coyote, or Ma'ii. Coyote is a trickster, a character who is both clever and foolish, wise and mischievous. His stories are filled with humor and often carry important lessons about human behavior and the consequences of one's actions. In one popular story, Coyote decides he wants to fly like the birds. He asks the birds to give him feathers, and they kindly agree. However, once he has enough feathers to fly, Coyote becomes arrogant and starts showing off, ignoring the birds' warnings. Eventually, the feathers fall off, and Coyote crashes to the ground. This story teaches the dangers of arrogance and the importance of listening to others.

Another important figure in Navajo legends is Spider Woman, or Na'ashjéii Asdzáá́. Spider Woman is a wise and nurturing deity who taught the Navajo people the art of weaving. According to legend, she created the first loom and showed the people how to weave intricate patterns that reflect the beauty and complexity of the world. Spider Woman's stories emphasize the importance of creativity, patience, and the interconnection of all things. She is a symbol of knowledge and skill, guiding the Navajo in their craft and daily lives.

The Hero Twins, Monster Slayer (Naayéé' Neizghání) and Born-for-Water (Tóbájíshchíní), are central figures in many Navajo stories. These twin brothers were born to Changing Woman and set out on a quest to rid the world of monsters that threatened their people. With the help of their father, the Sun God, and other Holy People, the twins embarked on numerous adventures, facing formidable foes and overcoming great challenges. Their stories are filled with excitement and teach lessons about bravery, perseverance, and the importance of working together. The Hero Twins symbolize the fight against adversity and the triumph of good over evil.

Changing Woman, or Asdzáá Nádleehi, is another key figure in Navajo mythology. She represents life, growth, and renewal. According to legend, Changing Woman was created by the Holy People and given the power to change her age from a young woman to an old woman and back again, symbolizing the cycles of life and nature. Her stories teach about the natural world, the importance of nurturing life, and the role of women in Navajo society. Changing Woman is revered for her strength and wisdom, embodying the enduring spirit of the Navajo people.

The Sun God, or Jóhonaa'éí, is a powerful deity who travels across the sky each day, bringing light and warmth to the world. His journey is a daily reminder of the passage of time and the cycles of nature. Stories about the Sun God emphasize his role as a protector and guide, providing light and life to all beings. The Sun God is often invoked in prayers and songs, seeking his blessings and guidance.

Water is also a significant element in Navajo folklore. Water spirits, known as Tó Neinilí, are believed to inhabit springs, rivers, and lakes. These spirits are revered and respected, and their presence is considered essential for life and growth. Stories about water spirits often highlight the importance of respecting and protecting water sources, teaching the Navajo to live in harmony with nature.

The natural world is deeply woven into Navajo legends and folklore. Animals, plants, and celestial bodies are often featured as characters, each with their own stories and significance. The eagle, for example, is seen as a messenger between the earthly and spiritual realms. Eagle stories teach lessons about vision, strength, and spiritual connection. The bear is another important figure, symbolizing courage and protection. Bear stories often emphasize the importance of respecting nature and understanding its power.

The stories and legends of the Navajo are not just for entertainment; they are educational tools that impart moral and ethical lessons. They teach children about their cultural heritage, guiding them in their understanding of the world and their place within it. Through these stories, the Navajo learn about their ancestors, the values of their community, and the importance of living in harmony with nature.

One of the ways these stories are shared is through oral tradition. Elders play a crucial role in this process, passing down stories from generation to generation. This oral tradition is a living, dynamic practice, with each storyteller bringing their own interpretation and style to the tales. Listening to these stories is a communal experience, bringing families and communities together and reinforcing their cultural bonds.

The storytelling tradition also includes songs, chants, and prayers. These oral practices are an integral part of Navajo ceremonies and rituals, invoking the presence of the Holy People and the spirits of nature. The words and melodies carry the power of the ancestors, connecting the Navajo to their history and their land. This oral tradition ensures that the knowledge and wisdom of the Navajo people are preserved and passed on to future generations.

Modern technology has provided new platforms for preserving and sharing Navajo stories and legends. Recordings of elders telling stories, digital archives, and online educational programs make these rich traditions accessible to a broader audience. These modern tools complement traditional practices, ensuring that the stories continue to be told and appreciated.

7 /
navajo food and agriculture

traditional navajo foods and recipes

ONE OF THE most iconic Navajo foods is fry bread, a simple yet delicious treat that holds a special place in Navajo culture. Fry bread is made from a basic dough of flour, water, salt, and baking powder, which is then fried to a golden perfection. The result is a crispy, fluffy bread that can be enjoyed on its own or used as a base for other dishes, such as Navajo tacos. The history of fry bread is intertwined with the Long Walk and the rations provided by the U.S. government, making it a symbol of resilience and adaptability.

To make fry bread, start by mixing two cups of flour, one teaspoon of salt, one teaspoon of baking powder, and a cup of water in a large bowl. Knead the dough until it is smooth, then let it rest for about 30 minutes. Divide the dough into small balls and flatten each one into a disc. Heat oil in a frying pan and fry each disc until it puffs up and turns golden brown, flipping once to ensure both sides are cooked. Serve the fry bread warm, with honey, powdered sugar, or as a base for savory toppings.

Another traditional Navajo dish is mutton stew, a hearty and flavorful soup that is perfect for cold days. Mutton, which comes from sheep, is a staple in Navajo cuisine, reflecting the importance of sheep herding in Navajo culture. The stew is made with tender pieces of mutton, potatoes, onions, and sometimes corn or other vegetables, all simmered together to create a rich and comforting meal.

To prepare mutton stew, start by cutting two pounds of mutton into bite-sized pieces. In a large pot, brown the mutton over medium heat until it develops a nice crust. Add a chopped onion and sauté until it becomes translucent. Then, add four cups of water, two diced potatoes, and any other vegetables you like, such as corn or carrots. Season with salt, pepper, and a pinch of dried juniper berries if you have them. Let the stew simmer for about an hour, or until the meat is tender and the flavors have melded together. Serve the stew hot, accompanied by fry bread or cornmeal mush.

Corn is another essential ingredient in Navajo cuisine, used in various forms and dishes. Blue corn mush is a traditional breakfast food made from ground blue cornmeal, water, and juniper ash, which gives it a distinctive flavor and nutritional boost. This simple dish is both nutritious and comforting, providing a warm start to the day.

To make blue corn mush, combine one cup of blue cornmeal with four cups of water in a saucepan. Add a pinch of salt and a small amount of juniper ash, which can be found at specialty stores or made at home by burning juniper branches and sifting the ashes. Bring the mixture to a boil, stirring constantly to prevent lumps. Reduce the heat and let it simmer until it thickens to a porridge-like consistency, about 10-15 minutes. Serve the mush warm, with a drizzle of honey or a sprinkle of sugar if desired.

Navajo tea, or greenthread tea, is a traditional beverage made from the wild herb Thelesperma, which grows in the Southwest. This tea has been enjoyed for generations, known for its mild, earthy flavor and soothing properties. Navajo tea is often consumed both for its taste and its potential health benefits, such as aiding digestion and promoting relaxation.

To brew Navajo tea, gather a handful of dried greenthread stems and leaves. Rinse them gently to remove any dust or debris. Boil four cups of water in a pot, then add the dried herbs. Let the tea steep for about 10 minutes, or until it reaches the desired strength. Strain the tea into cups and enjoy it hot or chilled, plain or with a touch of honey or lemon.

Sheep, as mentioned, are vital to Navajo culture, not only providing meat but also wool for weaving. Lamb is another common ingredient in Navajo dishes. Lamb and bean stew is a traditional dish that combines tender lamb with hearty beans and vegetables, creating a satisfying and nutritious meal.

To make lamb and bean stew, start by soaking one cup

of dried beans (such as pinto or kidney beans) overnight. Drain and rinse the beans, then set them aside. In a large pot, brown one pound of lamb pieces over medium heat. Add a chopped onion and a couple of minced garlic cloves, sautéing until fragrant. Add the soaked beans, four cups of water or broth, and any vegetables you like, such as diced tomatoes, carrots, and green chilies. Season with salt, pepper, and a teaspoon of ground cumin. Let the stew simmer for about an hour and a half, or until the beans and lamb are tender. Serve hot, with a side of fry bread or blue corn tortillas.

Hominy, made from dried corn kernels that have been treated with an alkali, is another staple in Navajo cooking. Hominy stew, also known as posole, is a traditional dish that combines hominy with pork or lamb, green chilies, and various spices. This hearty stew is packed with flavor and is often enjoyed during celebrations and communal gatherings.

To prepare hominy stew, start by browning one pound of pork or lamb pieces in a large pot. Add a chopped onion and sauté until soft. Then, add four cups of cooked hominy (or canned hominy, drained and rinsed), two cups of broth, and a couple of roasted and peeled green chilies, chopped. Season with salt, pepper, and a teaspoon of ground coriander. Let the stew simmer for about an hour, allowing the flavors to meld together. Serve the hominy stew hot, garnished with fresh cilantro and lime wedges.

farming and livestock practices

Farming has always been a cornerstone of Navajo life, with techniques and crops passed down through generations. Traditional Navajo farming focuses on crops that are well-suited to the arid climate of the Southwest. The "Three Sisters" – corn, beans, and squash – are central to Navajo agriculture. These crops are often planted together in a system called companion planting, where each plant supports the growth of the others. Corn provides a structure for the beans to climb, beans enrich the soil with nitrogen, and squash spreads out to cover the ground, helping to retain moisture and suppress weeds.

Planting and harvesting seasons are marked by ceremonies and rituals that honor the earth and seek blessings for a bountiful yield. These practices emphasize the importance of maintaining harmony with nature and respecting the land. The fields are often blessed with corn pollen, and songs and prayers are offered to ensure the health of the crops.

One traditional farming method used by the Navajo is dry farming. This technique relies on the careful conservation of moisture in the soil. Farmers plant crops in deep furrows or pits to capture and retain rainwater. Mulching with natural materials like straw or leaves helps to reduce evaporation and keep the soil cool. Dry farming is a testament to the ingenuity and adaptability of Navajo farmers, who have learned to thrive in a challenging environment.

In addition to the Three Sisters, Navajo farmers grow

other crops such as melons, sunflowers, and various herbs. Each plant has its own role in the diet and culture of the Navajo people. Sunflowers, for example, provide seeds that are a valuable food source, while their tall stalks can act as windbreaks to protect more delicate plants. Herbs are used not only in cooking but also in traditional medicine, highlighting the deep connection between agriculture and holistic health in Navajo culture.

Livestock farming is another integral part of Navajo life. Sheep, goats, cattle, and horses are all raised by Navajo families, each animal playing a crucial role in their economy and way of life. Sheep, in particular, hold a special place in Navajo culture. Sheep herding and wool weaving are traditional practices that have been passed down through generations. The wool from sheep is used to create beautiful and intricate textiles, such as rugs and blankets, which are highly valued both within and outside the Navajo community.

Tending to livestock involves daily routines that foster a strong bond between the Navajo people and their animals. Shepherds lead their flocks to grazing areas, ensuring they have access to fresh grass and water. The health and well-being of the animals are closely monitored, with practices in place to protect them from predators and harsh weather conditions. This close relationship with livestock reflects the Navajo belief in the interconnectedness of all life and the responsibility to care for and respect living beings.

Horses are also significant in Navajo culture, symbolizing freedom, strength, and mobility. Historically, horses have been essential for transportation, hunting, and trade. Today, they continue to play an important role in daily life and cultural practices. Horseback riding and racing are popular activities, and horses are often featured in ceremonies and celebrations.

Modern farming and livestock practices among the Navajo incorporate traditional knowledge with contemporary techniques. Many Navajo farmers and ranchers use modern tools and equipment to increase efficiency and productivity while still honoring traditional methods. For example, irrigation systems are used to supplement dry farming techniques, ensuring crops receive adequate water in an increasingly unpredictable climate. Sustainable farming practices, such as crop rotation and organic farming, are also embraced to protect the environment and preserve the health of the land.

Education and community support play crucial roles in sustaining Navajo farming and livestock practices. Agricultural programs and initiatives provide training and resources to Navajo farmers and ranchers, helping them to adopt new technologies and improve their practices. Community gardens and cooperative farming projects foster collaboration and knowledge sharing, strengthening the bonds within the community and ensuring the continuation of agricultural traditions.

Navajo farmers and ranchers face various challenges, including land and water rights issues, climate change, and economic pressures. However, their resilience and commitment to their cultural heritage drive them to find innovative solutions and advocate for their rights. Organizations such as the Navajo Nation Department of Agriculture work to support and protect the interests of Navajo farmers and ranchers, promoting sustainable practices and ensuring access to resources.

The importance of farming and livestock practices in Navajo culture extends beyond the practical need for food and resources. These practices are deeply intertwined with spiritual beliefs, social structures, and cultural identity. The act of planting, tending, and harvesting crops, as well as caring for livestock, is seen as a way to honor the earth and maintain harmony with the natural world. Through these activities, the Navajo people connect with their ancestors, their community, and their land.

8 / challenges and triumphs

the long walk and its impact

THE LONG WALK began in 1864, amidst increasing tensions between the Navajo and the United States government. The U.S. government, seeking to control the valuable lands of the Southwest, decided to forcibly relocate the Navajo people. Under the command of Colonel Kit Carson, the U.S. military was ordered to round up the Navajo and march them from their homelands in what is now Arizona and New Mexico to a desolate reservation at Bosque Redondo in eastern New Mexico.

Imagine being part of a community forced to leave your home with little more than what you could carry. Men, women, children, and the elderly were all compelled to make this arduous journey. The march covered over 300 miles, through harsh terrain and extreme weather conditions. Many Navajo had to walk the entire distance, enduring bitter cold, scorching heat, and constant hunger and thirst.

The journey was brutal. Along the way, the Navajo faced numerous hardships. They were given inadequate food and water, leading to malnutrition and dehydration. The elderly and the very young were particularly vulnerable, and many did not survive the journey. Disease spread rapidly among the people, further increasing the death toll. Families were torn apart, and the suffering was immense.

Upon reaching Bosque Redondo, the Navajo people found little solace. The land was barren and unsuitable for farming. The promised provisions were meager and often spoiled, leading to severe food shortages. The conditions at Bosque Redondo were dire. The water was contaminated, leading to further health issues. The Navajo struggled to grow crops in the poor soil, and their livestock, essential to their way of life, often perished.

Despite these harsh conditions, the Navajo people showed remarkable resilience. They continued to hold onto their cultural practices and traditions, finding ways to support each other and maintain their identity. The sense of community and solidarity among the Navajo was a source of strength during these dark times. They sang their traditional songs, told their stories, and kept their language alive, ensuring that their cultural heritage was preserved even in the face of adversity.

The suffering at Bosque Redondo did not go unnoticed. Reports of the appalling conditions reached Washington, and eventually, the U.S. government recognized the failure of the reservation experiment. In 1868, after four long years, the Navajo leaders, including the respected Manuelito, negotiated a treaty with the U.S. government. This treaty allowed the Navajo people to return to a portion of their ancestral lands. The joy and relief of returning home were tempered by the losses they had endured, but it marked the end of the Long Walk and the beginning of their recovery.

The impact of the Long Walk on the Navajo Nation was profound and long-lasting. The physical and emotional scars of this forced relocation were deeply felt by those who survived and were passed down through generations. The loss of lives, the disruption of their way of life, and the trauma of the journey left an indelible mark on the Navajo people.

Returning to their homeland was just the beginning of a long process of rebuilding. The Navajo had to start anew, reestablishing their communities and reclaiming their land. They faced numerous challenges in this process, including conflicts over land rights, the need to rebuild their agricultural practices, and the struggle to maintain their cultural traditions amidst pressures to assimilate into mainstream American society.

Despite these challenges, the Navajo people demonstrated incredible resilience and determination. They worked tirelessly to restore their communities and revive their cultural practices. The experience of the Long Walk reinforced their commitment to their land, their way of life, and their identity as a people. The memory of the Long Walk became a powerful symbol of their endurance and strength, a reminder of the hardships they had overcome and the resilience that defines them.

In contemporary Navajo culture, the Long Walk is commemorated and remembered through stories, ceremonies, and educational programs. It serves as a powerful reminder of the Navajo's resilience and the importance of preserving their cultural heritage. The lessons learned from this dark chapter in history continue to inspire and guide the Navajo people as they navigate the challenges of the modern world.

The story of the Long Walk also holds important lessons for all of us. It is a stark reminder of the injustices faced by indigenous peoples and the enduring impact of such events on their communities. It underscores the importance of understanding and acknowledging these historical events and supporting the efforts of indigenous communities to heal and thrive.

As we reflect on the Long Walk, we are reminded of the strength and resilience of the Navajo people. Their journey, marked by immense suffering and profound endurance, is a testament to their spirit and determination. By honoring their story and learning from their experiences, we can better appreciate the depth of their culture and the importance of preserving and respecting the rights and heritage of all indigenous peoples.

modern-day challenges and achievements

One of the significant challenges faced by the Navajo Nation is access to clean water. Despite being the largest Native American reservation in the United States, many Navajo communities lack reliable access to safe drinking water. This issue is compounded by the legacy of uranium mining, which has left parts of the land contaminated and water sources unsafe. Efforts to address this challenge involve both modern technology and traditional knowledge. Organizations and activists are working tirelessly to provide clean water solutions, from installing filtration systems to advocating for policy changes. These efforts are crucial for improving health outcomes and ensuring the well-being of future generations.

Another pressing issue is healthcare. The Navajo Nation has faced significant health disparities, including high rates of diabetes, heart disease, and other chronic illnesses. The COVID-19 pandemic highlighted these vulnerabilities, as the Navajo Nation experienced some of the highest infection rates in the country. In response, the Navajo community demonstrated remarkable resilience and solidarity. Grassroots organizations mobilized to provide essential supplies, healthcare workers went above and beyond to care for their communities, and traditional practices were incorporated into public health strategies. This collaborative spirit has not only helped to combat the immediate crisis but also strengthened the healthcare infrastructure for the future.

Education is another area where the Navajo Nation faces challenges but also sees significant achievements. Historically, education policies aimed at assimilating Native American children into mainstream society often stripped away their cultural identity. Today, there is a strong movement to reclaim and revitalize Navajo language and culture within the education system. Schools on the reservation are increasingly incorporating Navajo language programs, traditional teachings, and culturally relevant curricula. These efforts empower Navajo students to connect with their heritage while preparing for future opportunities. Additionally, higher education initiatives and scholarship programs are opening doors for Navajo youth to pursue advanced degrees and professional careers.

Economic development is crucial for the Navajo Nation's self-sufficiency and prosperity. Unemployment rates on the reservation have historically been high, and economic opportunities have been limited. However, there have been significant strides in diversifying the economy. Renewable energy projects, such as solar and wind farms, are providing sustainable energy and creating jobs. The Navajo Nation is also investing in tourism, leveraging its rich cultural heritage and breathtaking landscapes to attract visitors from around the world. These initiatives not only generate revenue but also foster a sense of pride and cultural preservation.

Environmental stewardship is deeply rooted in Navajo culture, and modern challenges have intensified the need for sustainable practices. The impact of climate change, including prolonged droughts and changing weather patterns, poses significant threats to traditional farming and livestock practices. In response, the Navajo Nation is embracing innovative approaches to environmental management. Water conservation techniques, soil regeneration projects, and community-based agriculture initiatives are helping to build resilience against climate change. These efforts reflect a harmonious blend of traditional knowledge and modern science, ensuring that the land can sustain future generations.

Political engagement and self-governance are also critical areas of focus for the Navajo Nation. The establishment of the Navajo Tribal Council in the 1920s marked a significant step towards self-governance. Today, the Navajo Nation has a robust governmental structure that addresses the needs and aspirations of its people. Political leaders advocate for the rights and interests of the Navajo at local, state, and national levels. Issues such as land rights, natural resource management, and sovereignty are central to their efforts. The active participation of the Navajo people in political processes underscores their commitment to self-determination and community empowerment.

Cultural preservation remains a cornerstone of Navajo life. The Navajo Nation is home to a wealth of cultural practices, from weaving and pottery to storytelling and traditional ceremonies. These cultural expressions are not only sources of pride but also vital components of the Navajo identity. Efforts to preserve and promote Navajo culture are evident in community events, cultural centers, and educational programs. Artisans, elders, and cultural practitioners play a crucial role in passing down these traditions, ensuring that they remain vibrant and relevant in the modern world.

Technology and digital connectivity have become essential tools for the Navajo Nation's progress. The digital divide has been a significant barrier, with many communities lacking reliable internet access. However, recent initiatives aim to bridge this gap. Investments in broadband infrastructure are enhancing educational opportunities, improving healthcare delivery through telemedicine, and fostering economic development through e-commerce and remote work. Digital platforms also provide a means to share and celebrate Navajo culture with a global audience, amplifying their voices and stories.

9 /
how you can help

ways to learn more about navajo culture

ONE OF THE most immersive ways to learn about Navajo culture is by visiting the Navajo Nation itself. Located in the Four Corners region of the United States, the Navajo Nation is home to stunning landscapes, from the red rock formations of Monument Valley to the serene beauty of Canyon de Chelly. These places are not only breathtaking but also deeply connected to Navajo history and spirituality. Guided tours led by Navajo guides offer an authentic perspective, sharing stories and insights that bring these landscapes to life. Visiting cultural sites such as the Navajo Nation Museum in Window Rock, Arizona, provides a comprehensive overview of Navajo history, art, and traditions.

Participating in cultural events and festivals is another enriching way to experience Navajo culture firsthand. The Navajo Nation Fair, held annually in Window Rock, is the

Sarah Michaels

largest Native American fair in the country. It features rodeos, parades, traditional dances, arts and crafts exhibitions, and much more. Attending such events allows you to witness and celebrate Navajo traditions, enjoy traditional foods, and engage with the community. These festivals are vibrant displays of Navajo pride and heritage, offering a unique opportunity to connect with the culture on a personal level.

If traveling to the Navajo Nation isn't possible, there are still many ways to learn from a distance. Books and literature provide a deep dive into Navajo culture, history, and contemporary issues. Works by Navajo authors such as N. Scott Momaday, Luci Tapahonso, and Laura Tohe offer profound insights into the Navajo experience. Reading fiction, poetry, and autobiographies written by Navajo authors helps to understand the culture from an insider's perspective. Additionally, books on Navajo history and anthropology, such as "The Navajo" by Aileen O'Bryan and "Dinétah: An Early History of the Navajo People" by Lawrence D. Sundberg, offer scholarly and accessible accounts of Navajo heritage.

For those who prefer visual and auditory learning, documentaries and films about the Navajo can be incredibly informative. Documentaries like "The Long Walk: Tears of the Navajo" and "We Shall Remain: The Navajo" provide historical context and personal stories that bring Navajo history to life. Films such as "The Return of Navajo Boy" offer a contemporary look at the Navajo Nation, addressing issues such as uranium mining and cultural preservation.

These visual mediums provide an engaging way to learn about Navajo culture and the challenges and triumphs of the Navajo people.

Online resources and digital platforms have made learning about Navajo culture more accessible than ever. Websites like the Navajo Nation Government's official site offer information on Navajo history, governance, and current events. Online courses and webinars hosted by universities and cultural organizations provide in-depth knowledge on specific aspects of Navajo culture, such as language, art, and traditional practices. Social media platforms also offer a way to connect with Navajo content creators, artists, and activists who share their experiences and perspectives.

Learning the Navajo language, Diné Bizaad, is a powerful way to connect with Navajo culture on a deeper level. Language is a vital component of cultural identity, and understanding even a few words or phrases can enhance your appreciation of Navajo traditions and worldview. There are numerous resources available for learning Navajo, from language classes offered by universities and community colleges to online courses and language apps. The Navajo Language Academy and the Diné College offer programs and materials for learners of all levels. Practicing the language with Navajo speakers, whether in person or through language exchange programs, can also be a rewarding experience.

Art and crafts are integral to Navajo culture, reflecting the creativity and traditions of the Navajo people. Exploring

Sarah Michaels

Navajo art, whether through galleries, museums, or online platforms, offers a window into the cultural expressions and stories that are woven into each piece. Navajo weaving, pottery, jewelry, and sand painting are renowned for their beauty and craftsmanship. Visiting galleries and exhibitions, such as those at the Heard Museum in Phoenix, Arizona, or the Museum of Indian Arts and Culture in Santa Fe, New Mexico, allows you to see these exquisite works up close and learn about the techniques and symbolism behind them.

Engaging with Navajo communities and organizations is another meaningful way to learn. Many Navajo non-profits and cultural organizations welcome volunteers and visitors who are interested in supporting their work and learning about Navajo culture. Organizations like the Navajo Nation Human Rights Commission and the Diné Cultural Center offer programs and events that educate and advocate for Navajo rights and culture. Volunteering or participating in community events provides an opportunity to build relationships and gain a deeper understanding of the Navajo way of life.

Educational institutions, both within and outside the Navajo Nation, offer courses and programs focused on Navajo studies. Diné College, the first tribally controlled and accredited collegiate institution in the United States, provides a range of programs in Navajo language, culture, and history. Other universities, such as Northern Arizona University and the University of New Mexico, offer courses in Native American studies with a focus on the Navajo.

Enrolling in these courses or attending lectures and seminars can provide a structured and comprehensive approach to learning about Navajo culture.

how to support the navajo nation

One of the most direct ways to support the Navajo Nation is through donations. Many Navajo families and communities face significant economic challenges, including high unemployment rates and limited access to essential resources. Donations to reputable Navajo non-profits and organizations can provide immediate relief and support long-term development projects. Organizations such as the Navajo Nation COVID-19 Relief Fund, Navajo & Hopi Families COVID-19 Relief Fund, and the Navajo Water Project focus on critical areas like healthcare, food security, and water access. Contributions to these organizations help provide clean water, medical supplies, food, and other essential resources to those in need.

Another impactful way to support the Navajo Nation is by purchasing Navajo-made goods. Navajo artisans are renowned for their exceptional craftsmanship in weaving, pottery, jewelry, and other traditional arts. By buying directly from Navajo artists, you not only support their livelihoods but also help preserve and promote Navajo cultural heritage. Online marketplaces, local craft fairs, and galleries that feature authentic Navajo art are great places to find unique and beautiful pieces. When purchasing Navajo goods, it's essential to ensure they are genuine and ethically sourced, supporting the artisans who create them.

Advocacy and raising awareness are also crucial. Educating yourself and others about the history, culture, and current issues facing the Navajo Nation helps to foster understanding and support. Sharing this knowledge through social media, community events, and educational programs can amplify the voices of the Navajo people and bring attention to their needs and achievements. Advocating for policies that support Native American rights and sovereignty at local, state, and national levels can lead to meaningful changes that benefit the Navajo Nation.

Volunteering your time and skills is another valuable way to support the Navajo Nation. Many organizations within the Navajo community welcome volunteers who can contribute to various projects and initiatives. Whether you have expertise in healthcare, education, construction, or environmental conservation, there are opportunities to make a difference. Volunteering can be a deeply rewarding experience, allowing you to build connections with the Navajo community and gain a deeper understanding of their culture and challenges.

Supporting Navajo education is critical for the future of the Navajo Nation. Donations to scholarship funds and educational programs help provide Navajo students with opportunities to pursue higher education and professional careers. Organizations such as the American Indian College Fund and the Navajo Nation Scholarship and Financial Assistance Program offer scholarships and support services to Navajo students. By contributing to these programs, you help empower the next generation of Navajo leaders and professionals.

Environmental stewardship is another important area where you can support the Navajo Nation. The Navajo land faces numerous environmental challenges, including water scarcity, pollution from mining activities, and the impacts of climate change. Supporting initiatives that focus on environmental protection and sustainability can have a lasting positive impact. Organizations like the Black Mesa Water Coalition and Diné CARE (Citizens Against Ruining our Environment) work to protect Navajo natural resources and promote sustainable practices. Contributions to these organizations support their efforts to ensure a healthy and sustainable environment for the Navajo people.

Building and maintaining respectful relationships with the Navajo community is foundational to meaningful support. Engaging with the Navajo Nation in ways that honor their sovereignty and cultural values fosters mutual respect and understanding. Attending cultural events, learning the Navajo language, and participating in community activities with a genuine spirit of respect and openness can strengthen these relationships. Listening to and valuing the perspectives and leadership of Navajo people is essential in any collaborative effort.

Supporting Navajo businesses is another way to make a positive impact. Many Navajo entrepreneurs are working to build sustainable businesses that provide goods and services within and beyond their community. By patronizing Navajo-owned businesses, you help boost the local economy and create job opportunities. Whether it's a restaurant, a craft shop, or a service provider, supporting these businesses contributes to the economic vitality of the Navajo Nation.

Advocating for improved healthcare access and services is critical. The Navajo Nation has faced significant healthcare disparities, which have been exacerbated by the COVID-19 pandemic. Supporting healthcare initiatives and advocating for policies that increase funding and resources for Navajo healthcare services can help address these disparities. Organizations like Partners In Health and Johns Hopkins Center for American Indian Health work to improve healthcare delivery and outcomes for the Navajo people. Supporting these organizations through donations or volunteering can make a substantial difference.

Engaging in cultural exchange programs can foster deeper connections and understanding. Programs that facilitate cultural exchange between Navajo communities and other groups help bridge gaps and build relationships based on mutual respect and learning. These exchanges can involve students, artists, professionals, and community members, creating opportunities for dialogue, collaboration, and shared experiences.

10 / fun activities and crafts

simple navajo-inspired crafts for kids

NAVAJO BEADED BRACELETS

Beaded jewelry is a beautiful aspect of Navajo craftsmanship. Creating beaded bracelets is a simple yet engaging activity that allows kids to explore patterns and colors while developing fine motor skills.

Materials Needed:
- Seed beads in various colors
- Elastic beading cord
- Scissors
- Bead needle (optional for younger kids)

Instructions:

Sarah Michaels

1. Choose Your Beads: Select a variety of seed beads in different colors. Think about the patterns and colors you want to use. Traditional Navajo colors include turquoise, red, black, and white, but you can choose any colors you like.

2. Measure the Cord: Cut a piece of elastic beading cord to fit your wrist, adding a couple of extra inches to make tying the knot easier.

3. String the Beads: Thread the beads onto the cord, creating patterns as you go. You can use a bead needle to make this step easier, especially for smaller beads.

4. Tie the Knot: Once you have enough beads to fit around your wrist, carefully tie the ends of the cord together in a secure knot. You might want to add a drop of glue to the knot for extra security.

5. Trim the Excess: Cut off any excess cord, leaving a small tail to ensure the knot doesn't come undone.

6. Wear and Share: Your Navajo-inspired bracelet is ready to wear! Make a few more to share with friends or family.

Navajo Sand Paintings

Sand painting is a traditional Navajo art form used in healing ceremonies. Creating sand paintings is a fun and educational activity that allows kids to explore this beautiful art form in a simplified way.

. . .

Materials Needed:
- Colored sand (or you can color your own using sand and food coloring)
- Glue
- Cardstock or heavy paper
- Pencils
- Small brushes or paintbrushes

Instructions:
1. Draw Your Design: Start by sketching a simple design on a piece of cardstock. Traditional designs often include symbols such as arrows, circles, and animals, but feel free to get creative.
2. Apply Glue: Use a small brush to apply glue to one section of your drawing at a time. This will help keep the sand from spreading to unwanted areas.
3. Sprinkle Sand: Carefully sprinkle colored sand onto the glued areas. Shake off the excess sand onto a tray or piece of paper to reuse it.
4. Repeat: Continue applying glue and sand until your entire design is covered. You can use different colors of sand to make your design vibrant and colorful.
5. Let It Dry: Allow your sand painting to dry completely before displaying it.

Navajo Loom Weaving

Weaving is an essential part of Navajo culture, traditionally used to create beautiful rugs and blankets. This simplified loom weaving activity lets kids experience the basics of weaving.

Materials Needed:
- Cardboard (to make a simple loom)
- Yarn in various colors
- Scissors
- A ruler
- A plastic needle or a piece of cardboard shaped like a needle

Instructions:
1. Create the Loom: Cut a piece of cardboard to your desired size. Using a ruler, mark small notches about half an inch apart along the top and bottom edges.
2. Warp the Loom: Take a piece of yarn and thread it through the notches, wrapping it around the back and forth across the cardboard. These vertical threads are called the warp.
3. Weave the Weft: Cut a long piece of yarn and thread it onto your needle. Weave the needle over and under the warp threads, going back and forth across the loom. Push each row of yarn down with your fingers or a comb to keep it tight.
4. Change Colors: To add variety, you can change yarn

colors. Simply tie a new piece of yarn to the end of the previous piece and continue weaving.

5. Finish the Weaving: When your weaving is complete, carefully cut the warp threads off the loom and tie them to secure the weaving.

6. Display Your Work: Your woven piece can be used as a small rug, wall hanging, or even a coaster.

Navajo Painted Rocks

Painting rocks with traditional Navajo designs is a fun and easy craft that combines creativity with cultural learning.

Materials Needed:
- Smooth rocks
- Acrylic paint or paint pens
- Brushes
- Sealer (optional)

Instructions:
1. Clean the Rocks: Make sure your rocks are clean and dry before starting.

2. Choose a Design: Decide on a design inspired by Navajo patterns, such as geometric shapes, animals, or symbols.

3. Paint the Rocks: Use paint or paint pens to create your

design on the rocks. Be creative and use different colors and patterns.

4. Seal the Rocks: Once the paint is dry, you can apply a sealer to protect your artwork.

5. Display or Gift: These painted rocks can be used to decorate your garden, home, or given as thoughtful gifts.

basic navajo words and phrases to learn

Greetings and Common Phrases

Let's start with some everyday greetings and phrases. These are the words you'll use when you meet someone or want to express basic courtesies.

1. Yá'át'ééh (yah-t-eh): This is the Navajo word for "hello" or "greetings." It's a versatile greeting that can be used any time of the day.

2. Hágoónee' (hah-goh-nee): This means "goodbye" and is often used to wish someone well until you meet again.

3. Aoo' (ah-oh): This simple word means "yes."

4. Dooda (doh-dah): This is the Navajo word for "no."

5. Ahéhee' (ah-heh-heh): This means "thank you." It's a polite expression of gratitude.

6. T'áá shoodí (tah-shoh-dee): This means "please."

. . .

Introducing Yourself

Introducing yourself is an important part of making new friends and building relationships. Here are some phrases to help you introduce yourself in Navajo:

1. Shí éí [your name] yinishyé (sh-ee ay [your name] yih-nih-sh-yeh): This means "My name is [your name]."
2. Nizhónígo nidaashch'ịị' (nih-zhoh-nee-goh nih-dahsh-ch'eeh): This means "Nice to meet you."

Numbers

Learning numbers in Navajo can be very helpful, especially if you're shopping, asking for directions, or simply practicing your language skills. Here are the numbers one through ten:

1. T'ááłá'í (t'ah-lah-ee): One
2. Naaki (nah-kee): Two
3. Táá' (tah): Three
4. Dį́į́' (dee): Four
5. Ashdla' (ahsh-dlah): Five
6. Hastą́ą́ (hahst-tah): Six

7. Tsosts'id (tsoh-ts'id): Seven
8. Tsee' (tseh): Eight
9. Náhást'éí (nah-hahst-ay): Nine
10. Nezní (nehz-nee): Ten

Days of the Week

Knowing the days of the week can help you talk about your plans and understand schedules. Here are the Navajo words for the days of the week:

1. Damóo (dah-moh): Sunday
2. Nahást'éí (nah-hahst-ay): Monday
3. Nahást'éí naaki (nah-hahst-ay nah-kee): Tuesday
4. Nahást'éí táá' (nah-hahst-ay tah): Wednesday
5. Nahást'éí dį́į́' (nah-hahst-ay dee): Thursday
6. Nahást'éí ashdla' (nah-hahst-ay ahsh-dlah): Friday
7. Nahást'éí hastą́ą́ (nah-hahst-ay hahst-tah): Saturday

Colors

Describing colors is useful in many situations, from talking about nature to describing your favorite things. Here are some basic colors in Navajo:

1. Łichíí' (łee-chee): Red
    2. Łigai (łih-gai): White
    3. Łitso (łih-tsoh): Yellow
    4. Dootł'izh (doot-łeezh): Blue
    5. Ch'ilgo dootł'izh (ch'il-goh doot-łeezh): Green
    6. Táá'nółts'ósí (tah-nil-tsoh-see): Black
    7. Łitsxo (łee-tsoh): Brown

Family Members

Talking about family is an important part of Navajo culture. Here are some words for family members:

1. Shimá (shih-mah): Mother
    2. Shizhé'é (shih-zheh-eh): Father
    3. Shádí (shah-dee): Older sister
    4. Shíye' (shih-yeh): Son
    5. Shideezhí (shih-deh-zhee): Younger sister
    6. Shitsilí (shih-tsee-lee): Younger brother
    7. Shitsilí (shih-tsee-lee): Grandchild

Animals

Sarah Michaels

Learning the names of animals can be fun and useful, especially if you're exploring the natural world. Here are some common animals in Navajo:

1. Mą'ii (mah-ee): Coyote
    2. Gah (gah): Rabbit
    3. Dibé (dih-beh): Sheep
    4. Tł'iish (tł'ee-sh): Snake
    5. Tł'iis (tł'ee-s): Horse
    6. Na'ashǫ́'ii (nah-ah-shoh-ee): Lizard
    7. Shash (shahsh): Bear
    8. Ch'osh (ch'ohsh): Bug

Basic Conversation Phrases

To help you get started with simple conversations, here are a few more phrases you might find helpful:

1. Hágoshį́į́' (hah-goh-shih): How are you?
    2. Yá'át'ééh abíní (yah-t-eh ah-bee-nee): Good morning
    3. Yá'át'ééh hiiłch'į' (yah-t-eh heel-ch'ee): Good evening
    4. Aoo', nizhóní (ah-oh, nih-zhoh-nee): Yes, it's beautiful
    5. Dooda, bilagáana t'áadoo (doh-dah, bih-lah-gah-nah tah-ah-doh): No, not a white person

. . .

Helpful Tips for Learning Navajo

Learning Navajo can be challenging but also incredibly rewarding. Here are some tips to help you along your journey:

1. Practice Regularly: Try to incorporate a few new words or phrases into your daily routine. Consistency is key to language learning.

2. Use Flashcards: Make flashcards with Navajo words on one side and the English translation on the other. This can help reinforce your memory.

3. Listen and Repeat: Listening to native speakers and repeating what they say can improve your pronunciation and understanding. There are many online resources and language apps that feature Navajo speakers.

4. Join a Language Group: Find a group of people who are also learning Navajo. Practicing with others can make learning more fun and effective.

5. Engage with the Culture: Learning a language is more than just words; it's about understanding the culture. Engage with Navajo culture through books, films, music, and conversations with Navajo people.

Sarah Michaels

recipes for traditional navajo snacks

Navajo Fry Bread

Navajo Fry Bread is perhaps the most iconic Navajo snack. It's a versatile dish that can be enjoyed plain, with sweet toppings, or as the base for savory dishes like Navajo Tacos.

Ingredients:
- 2 cups all-purpose flour
- 1 tablespoon baking powder
- 1 teaspoon salt
- 1 cup warm water
- Oil for frying (vegetable or canola oil works well)

Instructions:

1. Mix the Dough: In a large bowl, combine the flour, baking powder, and salt. Gradually add the warm water, mixing until a dough forms. The dough should be soft but not sticky.

2. Knead the Dough: Turn the dough onto a floured surface and knead for about 5 minutes until smooth and elastic.

3. Let It Rest: Cover the dough with a clean towel and let it rest for about 30 minutes. This helps it to rise slightly and become more pliable.

4. Heat the Oil: In a large frying pan, heat about an inch of oil over medium-high heat until it reaches 350°F (175°C).

5. Shape the Dough: Divide the dough into 8 equal pieces. Flatten each piece into a disc about 1/4 inch thick. Use your fingers to gently stretch and shape the discs.

6. Fry the Bread: Carefully place the dough discs into the hot oil, one or two at a time. Fry until golden brown, about 1-2 minutes per side. Use tongs to flip them and ensure even cooking.

7. Drain and Serve: Remove the fry bread from the oil and drain on paper towels. Serve warm with your favorite toppings, such as honey, powdered sugar, or savory fillings.

Blue Corn Mush

Blue Corn Mush is a traditional Navajo breakfast dish, but it also makes a great snack. It's made with blue cornmeal, which gives it a unique flavor and color.

Ingredients:
- 1 cup blue cornmeal
- 4 cups water
- 1/2 teaspoon salt
- Juniper ash (optional, for traditional flavor)
- Honey or sugar (optional, for sweetness)

. . .

Instructions:

1. Prepare the Ash Water (if using): If you have juniper ash, dissolve a small amount in warm water and let it settle. Use the clear liquid as your water base.

2. Boil the Water: In a large pot, bring the water (or ash water) to a boil.

3. Add the Cornmeal: Gradually add the blue cornmeal to the boiling water, stirring constantly to prevent lumps.

4. Cook the Mush: Reduce the heat to low and simmer the mixture, stirring frequently, until it thickens to a porridge-like consistency. This should take about 10-15 minutes.

5. Season and Serve: Stir in the salt. Serve the blue corn mush warm, with honey or sugar if you prefer a sweeter taste.

Navajo Popcorn (Toasted Pinon Nuts)

Pinon nuts, or pine nuts, are a traditional Navajo snack that can be enjoyed on their own or added to other dishes for extra flavor.

Ingredients:
- 1 cup pinon nuts (pine nuts)
- 1 tablespoon olive oil
- Salt to taste

Instructions:

1. Heat the Pan: In a medium skillet, heat the olive oil over medium heat.

2. Toast the Nuts: Add the pinon nuts to the skillet and toast, stirring constantly, until they are golden brown and fragrant. This should take about 5-7 minutes.

3. Season and Serve: Remove the nuts from the heat and season with salt to taste. Let them cool slightly before enjoying them as a snack.

Navajo Corn Cookies

These cookies are made with blue cornmeal and are a sweet, traditional treat that's perfect for snack time.

Ingredients:
- 1 cup blue cornmeal
- 1 cup all-purpose flour
- 1/2 teaspoon baking soda
- 1/2 teaspoon salt
- 1/2 cup unsalted butter, softened
- 1/2 cup sugar
- 1/2 cup brown sugar
- 1 egg

Sarah Michaels

- 1 teaspoon vanilla extract

Instructions:

1. Preheat the Oven: Preheat your oven to 350°F (175°C). Line a baking sheet with parchment paper.

2. Mix the Dry Ingredients: In a medium bowl, combine the blue cornmeal, flour, baking soda, and salt. Set aside.

3. Cream the Butter and Sugars: In a large bowl, beat the softened butter, sugar, and brown sugar until light and fluffy.

4. Add the Egg and Vanilla: Beat in the egg and vanilla extract until well combined.

5. Combine the Mixtures: Gradually add the dry ingredients to the wet ingredients, mixing until just combined.

6. Shape the Cookies: Scoop tablespoon-sized portions of dough and place them on the prepared baking sheet, spacing them about 2 inches apart.

7. Bake: Bake the cookies for 10-12 minutes, or until the edges are golden brown. Allow them to cool on the baking sheet for a few minutes before transferring them to a wire rack to cool completely.

Navajo Tea (Greenthread Tea)

. . .

Navajo Tea is made from greenthread, a plant native to the Southwest. This traditional beverage is both refreshing and soothing.

Ingredients:
- A handful of dried greenthread stems and leaves
- 4 cups water
- Honey or lemon (optional)

Instructions:

1. Boil the Water: In a large pot, bring the water to a boil.

2. Brew the Tea: Add the dried greenthread to the boiling water. Reduce the heat and let it simmer for about 10 minutes.

3. Strain and Serve: Strain the tea into cups. Add honey or lemon if desired for extra flavor. Enjoy hot or chilled.

glossary

Diné (dee-neh)

Diné is the term the Navajo people use to refer to themselves. It means "The People" and reflects their identity and connection to their history, culture, and land. While "Navajo" is commonly used, "Diné" is preferred within the community and carries deeper cultural significance.

Navajo Nation

The Navajo Nation is the largest Native American reservation in the United States, covering approximately 27,000 square miles across Arizona, New Mexico, and Utah. It is a sovereign entity with its own government, laws, and services, providing a home for over 300,000 members.

Hózhó (hoh-zho)

Hózhó is a fundamental concept in Navajo culture, often translated as "beauty," "balance," or "harmony." It encompasses living in harmony with oneself, others, and the environment. Hózhó is about finding balance and walking in

Glossary

beauty, guiding the Navajo in their daily lives and spiritual practices.

Kinaaldá (kih-nahld-ah)

Kinaaldá is the traditional coming-of-age ceremony for Navajo girls, marking their transition into womanhood. It involves various rituals, including running, baking a corn cake called "alkan," and receiving guidance from elder women. This ceremony emphasizes community support, cultural teachings, and the importance of maintaining balance and harmony.

Diné Bizaad (dee-neh bih-zahd)

Diné Bizaad is the Navajo language. Preserving and revitalizing Diné Bizaad is crucial for maintaining Navajo culture and identity. Efforts to teach and promote the language include educational programs, media, and community initiatives.

Sheep and Weaving

Sheep herding and weaving are integral parts of Navajo culture and economy. Sheep provide wool, which Navajo weavers use to create beautiful, intricate rugs and blankets. Weaving is a revered art form passed down through generations, reflecting stories, traditions, and skills.

Hogan (hoh-gahn)

A Hogan is a traditional Navajo dwelling made from wooden poles, mud, and tree bark. There are two main types: the male Hogan, used for ceremonies and communal gatherings, and the female Hogan, used as a family home. The Hogan symbolizes harmony with nature and serves as a sacred space.

Glossary

Churro Sheep

Navajo-Churro sheep are a heritage breed brought to the Southwest by Spanish settlers. The Navajo adopted and adapted these sheep, which are valued for their hardy nature and long, lustrous wool. Churro wool is preferred for traditional weaving due to its durability and texture.

Navajo Code Talkers

During World War II, the Navajo Code Talkers were a group of Navajo Marines who created an unbreakable code based on the Navajo language. This code was used to transmit secure military communications and played a vital role in the Allied victory. The Code Talkers are celebrated heroes, symbolizing bravery and ingenuity.

Sand Painting

Sand painting is a traditional Navajo art form used in healing ceremonies. Using colored sand, artists create intricate, temporary designs that symbolize balance and harmony. These paintings are believed to invoke the powers of the Holy People for healing and protection.

The Long Walk (Hwéeldi)

The Long Walk refers to the forced relocation of the Navajo people in 1864 by the U.S. government. Thousands of Navajo were marched from their homelands to Bosque Redondo, a harsh and barren reservation. This traumatic event is a significant part of Navajo history, symbolizing resilience and the struggle for survival.

Blessingway Ceremony

The Blessingway is a Navajo ceremony that seeks to bring about good fortune, health, and blessings. It involves

Glossary

prayers, songs, and rituals to promote harmony and balance. This ceremony is often performed for significant life events, such as births, marriages, and journeys.

Diné Bikéyah (dee-neh bih-kay-yah)

Diné Bikéyah, meaning "Navajo Land," refers to the traditional and ancestral lands of the Navajo people. This land is central to Navajo identity and culture, encompassing sacred sites, historical places, and natural resources vital to their way of life.

Corn Pollen (Tádídíín)

Corn pollen, or Tádídíín, is used in many Navajo ceremonies and rituals. It represents life, growth, and fertility, symbolizing the connection between the Navajo people and the earth. Corn pollen is sprinkled during prayers and blessings to invoke protection and harmony.

Yá'át'ééh (yah-t-eh)

Yá'át'ééh is a common greeting in the Navajo language, meaning "hello" or "it is good." It is used to convey goodwill and respect when meeting someone. This greeting reflects the importance of positive connections and relationships in Navajo culture.

Mother Earth and Father Sky

In Navajo belief, Mother Earth (Nahasdzáán) and Father Sky (Yádiłhił) are central deities representing the natural world. They are honored in ceremonies and daily life, symbolizing the balance and interconnectedness of all creation. Respecting and caring for the earth and sky is a core value in Navajo spirituality.

Hataalii (ha-tah-lee)

Glossary

A Hataalii is a Navajo medicine person or healer. Hataaliis perform traditional ceremonies, including chants, sand paintings, and herbal remedies, to heal physical and spiritual ailments. They are highly respected figures in Navajo society, possessing deep knowledge of cultural and spiritual practices.

Spider Woman (Na'ashjé'ii Asdzą́ą́)

Spider Woman is a significant figure in Navajo mythology, known for teaching the Navajo people the art of weaving. She symbolizes creativity, wisdom, and the interconnectedness of life. Spider Woman's teachings are reflected in the intricate designs and patterns of Navajo textiles.

The Four Sacred Mountains

The Four Sacred Mountains define the traditional boundaries of Navajo land and hold spiritual significance. These mountains are Mount Blanca (Sisnaajiní), Mount Taylor (Tsoodził), the San Francisco Peaks (Dook'o'oosłíí́d), and Mount Hesperus (Dibé Nitsaa). They represent the cardinal directions and serve as symbols of protection and guidance.

further reading and resources

Websites to Explore

1. Navajo Nation Government Website

The official Navajo Nation website (https://www.navajo-nsn.gov) offers a wealth of information about the Navajo government, culture, history, and current events. It's a great resource for understanding how the Navajo Nation operates today.

2. Discover Navajo

The Discover Navajo website (https://discovernavajo.com) provides information about Navajo culture, tourism, and attractions. It's an excellent site for kids to learn about places they can visit within the Navajo Nation and the significance of these sites.

3. Navajo Code Talkers

The Navajo Code Talkers website (http://navajocodetalkers.org) is dedicated to the heroic Navajo Code Talkers of World War II. It includes stories, videos, and

Further Reading and Resources

educational resources that highlight their contributions and bravery.

4. PBS Learning Media: Native American Heritage

PBS offers a collection of educational resources about Native American cultures, including the Navajo. The site (https://www.pbslearningmedia.org/collection/native-american-heritage) features videos, lesson plans, and interactive activities suitable for kids.

5. National Museum of the American Indian

The Smithsonian's National Museum of the American Indian (https://americanindian.si.edu) has online exhibitions and resources about various Native American tribes, including the Navajo. The site includes engaging content for children, such as virtual tours and educational games.

Other Resources

1. YouTube Channels

- CrashCourse: CrashCourse offers educational videos on a variety of topics, including history and culture. Their videos on Native American history provide context and details about the Navajo Nation.

- Smithsonian Channel: The Smithsonian Channel features documentaries and short videos about Native American cultures. These videos can provide visual and narrative context to complement what kids read.

2. Documentaries and Films

- "We Shall Remain": This PBS series includes episodes on various Native American tribes, with one focusing specifically on the Navajo. It's a powerful way to see history and culture through storytelling and interviews.

Further Reading and Resources

- "The Long Walk: Tears of the Navajo": This documentary provides an in-depth look at the Long Walk and its impact on the Navajo people. It's a great visual companion to the book by Joseph Bruchac.

3. Museums and Cultural Centers

- Navajo Nation Museum: Located in Window Rock, Arizona, the Navajo Nation Museum (https://www.navajonationmuseum.org) has exhibits and educational programs that are accessible online. It's a fantastic resource for kids to explore Navajo artifacts and history.

- Heard Museum: The Heard Museum in Phoenix, Arizona (https://heard.org), features extensive collections and exhibits on Native American cultures, including the Navajo. Their website offers virtual exhibits and educational resources for children.

4. Language Learning Apps

- Navajo Language Renaissance: This organization offers apps and online resources to help learn the Navajo language. Learning some basic Navajo phrases can be a fun and interactive way for kids to connect with the culture.

5. Craft Kits

- Navajo Craft Kits: Craft kits that include materials and instructions for traditional Navajo crafts can be found online. These kits provide a hands-on learning experience, allowing kids to create their own Navajo-inspired art.

Educational Activities

1. Create a Navajo-Inspired Art Project

Kids can explore Navajo art by creating their own sand paintings, weaving projects, or beadwork. These activities help them understand the importance of these crafts in Navajo culture while expressing their creativity.

2. Cooking Navajo Recipes

Try making traditional Navajo foods like fry bread or blue corn mush. Cooking these recipes can be a fun way to learn about Navajo culinary traditions and the significance of food in their culture.

3. Virtual Field Trips

Many museums and cultural centers offer virtual field trips that allow kids to explore Navajo exhibits from home. These interactive tours can provide a dynamic learning experience and spark further interest in Navajo culture.

Milton Keynes UK
Ingram Content Group UK Ltd.
UKHW021410081224
452111UK00008B/182

9 798330 619146